The Emergence of
Noopolitik

*Toward an American
Information Strategy*

John Arquilla
David Ronfeldt

Prepared for the
Office of the Secretary of Defense

National Defense
Research Institute

RAND

PREFACE

This report builds on what we have accomplished so far in a set of studies, since 1991, about future military affairs (cyberwar), societal-level conflict and crime (netwar), and information strategy (see the Bibliography for relevant citations). Here we advance the idea of "noopolitik" (nü-oh-poh-li-teek), a new approach to statecraft based principally on the primacy of ideas, values, laws, and ethics, as enabled by the emergence of the noosphere (an all-encompassing realm of the mind), to extend our research agenda in a new direction.

Primarily of interest to U.S. policymakers and strategists, this report will also interest those in academia and think tanks concerned with how the information revolution is altering the conditions for and conduct of strategy.

This study was prepared for a project on information strategy. The project was sponsored by the Office of the Assistant Secretary of Defense/Command, Control, Communications, and Intelligence (OASD/C3I), and was conducted within both the Acquisition and Technology Policy Center and the International Security and Defense Policy Center of RAND's National Defense Research Institute (NDRI). NDRI is a federally funded research and development center sponsored by the Office of the Secretary of Defense, the Joint Staff, the Unified Commands, and the defense agencies.

John Arquilla
U.S. Naval Postgraduate School
Monterey, CA 93943
(408) 656-3450
jarquilla@nps.navy.mil

David Ronfeldt
RAND
Santa Monica, CA 90407-2138
(310) 393-0411
ronfeldt@rand.org

CONTENTS

FIGURE

TABLES

Information and communications have always been important to strategy. But they are changing from subsidiary to singular concerns—"information" matters more than ever for reasons that did not exist even 20 years ago. One reason is technological innovation: the growth of a vast new information infrastructure—including not only the Internet, but also cable systems, direct broadcast satellites, cellular phones, etc.—in which the balance is shifting away from one-to-many broadcast media (e.g., traditional radio and television) toward many-to-many interactive media. In many nations a growing, though varied, population is enjoying an ease of entry and access to the new infrastructure for commercial, social, diplomatic, military, and other interactions. This easy access is resulting in a huge increase in global interconnectivity.

A second reason is the proliferation of new organizations: Vast arrays of state and nonstate organizations are emerging that directly concern information and communications issues. A third reason why information and communications have become more important is that "information" and "power" are becoming increasingly intertwined. Across many political, economic, and military areas, informational "soft power" is taking precedence over traditional, material "hard power."

The new field known as "information strategy" is emerging around two poles, which define opposite ends of a spectrum of security concerns. One is an essentially technological pole, that of cyberspace safety and security. The other pole is essentially political and ideational—information strategy is seen as a way to harness and express the "soft power" of American democratic and market ideals, to attract, influence, and lead others.

Of the two poles, the technological one has received far more attention. Thus, there is an imbalance in current efforts to frame an American information strategy. Both poles are important. Yet, the concerns that encompass the technological pole have received the bulk of attention and appear to be well on the way to being figured out. The ideational pole is now the one more in need of work and clarification. Moreover, the technological and ideational poles should be linked together by strategic analysis that bridges the gap between them.

Such strategic thinking should impel a shift in American grand strategy, a shift growing out of and led by the rising importance of information strategy. In our view, a new paradigm is needed—in fact, it is already emerging—which we call *noopolitik* (nü-oh-poh-li-teek). This is the form of statecraft that we argue will come to be associated with the noosphere, the broadest informational realm of the mind (from the Greek *noos)* under which cyberspace (i.e., the Net) and the infosphere (cyberspace plus the media) are subsumed.

Noopolitik is foreign-policy behavior for the information age that emphasizes the primacy of ideas, values, norms, laws, and ethics—it would work through "soft power" rather than "hard power." Noopolitik is guided more by a conviction that right makes for might, than by the obverse. Both state and nonstate actors may be guided by noopolitik; but rather than being state-centric, its strength may likely stem from enabling state and nonstate actors to work conjointly. The driving motivation of noopolitik cannot be national interests defined in statist terms. National interests will still play a role, but they may be defined more in societywide than state-centric terms and be fused with broader, even global, interests in enhancing the transnationally networked "fabric" in which the players are embedded. While realpolitik tends to empower states, noopolitik will likely empower networks of state and nonstate actors. Realpolitik pits one state against another, but noopolitik encourages states to cooperate in coalitions and other mutual frameworks.

Noopolitik will not likely supplant the existing realpolitik paradigm of power politics in the near future. Rather the two forms will coexist, in an often rough, edgy balance that will vary regionally—because patterns of development remain uneven around the world. Some areas are already quite steeped in the dynamics of the information age, while others still seem more medieval than modern. Thus, noopolitik will be more pertinent in some parts of the world than in others, and in regard to some issues more than others.

We surmise that noopolitik will be most pertinent where technologically advanced societies predominate: e.g., parts of Western Europe and North America. It will be less so where conditions remain traditionally state-centric, and thus ripe for the continuation of realpolitik (e.g., much of Asia). Moreover, noopolitik will be most effective where all manner of media are prevalent, nongovernmental organizations (NGOs)[1] have an edge in generating attention to issues, the issues are complex rather than strictly economic or political or military, and where government-NGO relations are good.

The following measures could encourage construction of a global noosphere that would be of interest to all realms of society. They also embody a mix of measures to favor openness, on one hand, and protection, on the other. In this regard, they capture the essence of our preferred strategy for the United States—"guarded openness."

- Continue to support worldwide access to cyberspace. Support the access of NGOs as well as state and market actors to it, including where this runs counter to the preferences of authoritarian regimes.

- Move away from realpolitik-oriented designs to control encryption, and move toward freedom of encryption.

- To assure cyberspace safety and security at the international level, develop multitiered information systems for conditional information sharing, creating a shared—but still secure—infosphere.

---

[1]A word of clarification: NGOs are, for the most part, civil-society organizations. The point has been made to us several times by devotees of economic power that private, for-profit, commercial corporations are powerful NGOs. But this is incorrect usage. Such corporations are nonstate actors but not NGOs—that term (and acronym) apparently dates from the early years of the United Nations and was not meant to include commercial corporations. Neither was a related term, international nongovernmental organization (INGO), which we do not use here.

- Promote freedom of information and communications as a right (and responsibility) around the world.

- Encourage the creation of "special media forces," modeled along the lines of special forces units but armed with the weapons of the media rather than those of the military. These squads could be dispatched into conflict zones to help settle disputes through the discovery and dissemination of accurate information.

- Open up diplomacy to greater coordination between state and nonstate actors, especially NGOs, by undertaking a "revolution in diplomatic affairs" that matches the revolutions under way in business and military affairs.

In addition to building a global noosphere, it might also be advisable for the U.S. government to work on constructing a military noosphere that, emphasizing jointness and sharing, would span the U.S. services and allied and other friendly forces around the world. However, the balance between openness and guardedness might have to be different in a military noosphere from what it should be in a general global noosphere.

In the immediate future, to deal with a world in which noopolitik is emerging but strong elements of realpolitik persist, there is a need to prepare for information-age conflict by developing a strategic information doctrine (SID) to guide policy in crisis and conflict. Composed of "depth defenses" (i.e., layered electronic defenses against hackers), but also of proactive elements (electronic measures for going on the offensive), a SID should emphasize the guidance of the moral dimensions of noopolitik. This emphasis implies a policy of "no first use" of information weapons, which would allow the United States to "do good" in terms of decreasing the likelihood of information-age conflict—but also to "do well" by mitigating its own vulnerabilities to attack in cyberspace, where it has more information targets than almost any other entity.

Finally, we urge a shift from focusing on an "electronic Pearl Harbor" to aspiring to the benefits of an American-inspired information-age "Manifest Destiny."

ACKNOWLEDGMENTS

Once again, we are especially grateful to Captain Richard O'Neill (U.S. Navy, now retired) at the Office of the Assistant Secretary of Defense/Command, Control, Communications, and Intelligence (OASD/C3I) for his interest, support, and guidance. We are also grateful for encouraging comments and other guidance from OASD/C3I personnel Captain Gregory Blackburn (U.S. Navy), Lieutenant Colonel Robert Walter (U.S. Army), and Commander Bob Scott (U.S. Navy). In addition, we are indebted to Dr. John Hamre (Deputy Secretary of Defense) for his insightful comments on an earlier version of this study.

We are thankful to a number of members of the Highlands Forum, a consortium of government, business, academic, and media leaders devoted to the study of information-age issues, for the insightful comments they provided about some of the ideas we advance in this study. Finally, we benefited from thoughtful review comments provided by our RAND colleagues Robert Anderson and Greg Treverton and from skillful editing by Christina Pitcher.

Chapter One

WHITHER "INFORMATION STRATEGY"?

Something unsettling is happening to grand strategy. National security experts have long based their calculations on the traditional political, economic, and military dimensions of power. Now they see that a new field is emerging: "information strategy." Although still inchoate, it promises to redefine these three traditional dimensions. Moreover, it promises to seed the creation of a fourth—the "information" dimension, which is broadly understood to include technological conduits and conceptual contents. The world is turning anew into a highly charged battleground of ideas; it is not just a world in which material resources are the objects of protracted, often violent competition. In this emerging world, the key to success will likely lie in managing informational capabilities and resources skillfully—i.e., strategically.

Information strategy remains difficult to define and bound with precision, but the issues and debates shaping its appeal have been clustering around two poles for the past several years. One pole is basically technological: that of cyberspace safety and security. What drives concerns here is a sense of the vulnerability of essential U.S. information infrastructures to various forms of attack, especially by malicious actors who are skilled at launching cyberspace-based threats. Worrying how to defend against attacks by adversarial regimes, terrorists, and criminals, and wondering how to use cyberspace for counteroffensive attacks—that is what this pole is largely about. (See Hundley and Anderson, 1994; Molander, Riddile, and Wilson, 1996; and Campen, Dearth, and Goodden, 1996.)

1

The other pole is concerned with the politics of ideas—information strategy is seen as a way to harness and express the "soft power" of American ideals, so as to attract, influence, and lead others (Nye, 1990; Nye and Owens, 1996). The debates here are mainly about the benefits to be gained by opening and sharing our information and related information infrastructures with our allies and others, in such areas as intelligence and coalition formation. Moreover, there is a strong, optimistic emphasis on the media's roles in shaping people's views, as well as the Internet's. Broad strategies, involving the media more than cyberspace, are envisaged for using "information power" to promote democracies and constrain authoritarian regimes abroad. Thus, opportunities rather than threats are the motivating concerns.

Of the two poles, the technological one has received far more attention. Numerous conferences and gaming exercises have been held about "information warfare." A growing body of studies—think-tank analyses, congressional hearings, and a presidential commission— are serving to identify the key technological risks and vulnerabilities. Options are emerging, and interagency mechanisms (e.g., the National Infrastructure Protection Center) are taking shape for instituting systemic and nodal defenses to protect America's national and global information infrastructures and strategic subsystems.

Despite this considerable progress, inspection of the debates that are evolving around the more technical issues indicates that the technological pole cannot provide a sole basis for the formulation of information strategy. The debates remain largely about cyberspace-based vulnerabilities, and the ensuing language and scenarios tend to recapitulate old nuclear and terrorist paradigms that place heavy emphasis on potential worst-case threats (e.g., an "electronic Pearl Harbor"). All this is needed—indeed, infrastructure protection must be a priority of the U.S. government and private sector.[1] But this is far from adequate, even for developing the technological dimension as a

---

[1]For a recent discussion, see Smith, (*Issues in Science and Technology*), and the replies posted in the Forum section of the Winter 1998 issue of that journal by John J. Hamre (Deputy Secretary of Defense), Michael A. Vatis (chief, National Infrastructure Protection Center), and Arthur K. Cebrowski (Vice Admiral, U.S. Navy, and President, Naval War College). All this is available by following links at http://205.130.85.236/ issues/index.html/.

basis for information strategy writ large. Analysts must look beyond infrastructure defense; more is at stake in cyberspace than just technological vulnerability. They must look beyond risks, too, to help clarify the opportunities.

Meanwhile, less attention has been given to the development of soft power as a basis for information strategy. Strategists rarely convene to discuss it, and its influence is measured mainly by a small number of publications. True, there have been numerous conferences and studies about the changing roles of the media, public diplomacy, and intelligence in the information age. But a strategist interested in soft power as a basis for information strategy must pull these pieces together—they are rarely presented and analyzed as a coherent whole. The options in this area are not spelled out very well.

More to the point, the communities of experts associated with either the technological or the idea-sharing area do not meet much with those of the other. Both communities are aware of each other and share some common notions. For example, both communities presumably agree (with Nye and Owens, 1996, p. 35) that

> [i]nformation is the new coin of the international realm, and the United States is better positioned than any other country to multiply the potency of its hard and soft power resources through information.

Nevertheless, they remain disparate, insular communities, with few bridges connecting them.

Thus, there is an imbalance in current efforts to frame an American information strategy. Both poles are important. Yet, the concerns encompassing the technological pole have received the bulk of attention and appear to be well on the way to resolution. The sociopolitical dimension of idea sharing is now the one in need of much more work and clarification.

Further, the technological and ideational aspects should be linked by strategic analysis. Letting them develop separately along their current trajectories may lead to regrettable omissions of analysis. For example, narrow technical concern about cyber-terrorists who might take "the Net" down misses the strategic possibility that, politically, terrorists might prefer to leave the Net up, so as to spread their own soft-power message or engage in deception or intelligence gathering. On the other hand, enthusiasm about spreading American ideas may cause the United States to overlook the possibility that adversaries may exploit the media, the Internet, and other communications technologies to their own advantage.

However, more is at stake than omissions of analysis. Developing the technological and ideational dimensions of information technology together—rather than allowing them to take separate paths—will garner great opportunities. It is a mistake to think that these two poles represent an unremitting dichotomy rather than two parts of the same whole. Good ideas and options are needed for bridging and uniting them to create a broad, integrated vision of what American information strategy can become. We propose to unfold such a vision.

We begin by reconceptualizing the information realm. First, we argue that existing notions of cyberspace and the infosphere (cyberspace plus the media) should be seen as subsets of a broader "noosphere"—or globe-girdling realm of the mind. Advanced by the French scientist and clergyman Pierre Teilhard de Chardin in the mid-20th century, this concept is being rekindled by visionaries from a variety of quarters and can be of service to information strategists. In addition to recommending adoption of the concept of the noosphere, we suggest the need to shift from the current emphasis on "information processing" (a technology-oriented activity) to thinking also about "information structuring" (which emphasizes issues related to ideas and organization).

Our discussion of the noosphere anticipates the next key proposal: At the highest levels of statecraft, the development of information strategy may foster the emergence of a new paradigm, one based on ideas, values, and ethics transmitted through soft power—as opposed to power politics and its emphasis on the resources and capabilities associated with traditional, material "hard power." Thus, *realpolitik* (politics based on practical and material factors—those of, say, Henry Kissinger) will give some ground to what we call *noopoli-*

tik (nü-oh-poh-li-teek[2]—politics based on ethics and ideas, which we associate with many of those of George Kennan). As noopolitik emerges, the two approaches to statecraft will coexist for some decades. Sometimes they will complement each other, but often they will make for contradictory options. At first, information strategy may well serve in subordinate ways to traditional power politics—but, in our view, this will become ever less the case. Statesmen will always have recourse to traditional forms of power, but they will increasingly see benefits in emphasizing strategies that take advantage of informational means first, with force placed in a complementary role. This will work especially well when ethical notions form a key part of an information strategy approach to conflict, and when the initiative can come from either nonstate or state actors.

Strategy, at its best, knits together ends and means, no matter how various and disparate, into a cohesive pattern. In the case of an American information strategy, this requires balancing the need to guard and secure access to many informational capabilities and resources, with the opportunity to achieve national aims by fostering as much openness as practicable in the international system. Of course, an American strategy that supports a substantial amount of openness is sure to base itself on the assumption that greater interconnectivity leads to more liberal political development—an updated version of Lipset's (1960) "optimistic equation," which saw democracy moving in tandem with prosperity. Even so, it may be prudent to hedge against atavistic tendencies (e.g., an information-age totalitarianism) by means of continuing guardedness. Our term to represent such a strategic balancing act is "guarded openness," which we will discuss further in this report.

Building upon this foundation, we next examine the strategic information dimensions of two key areas that bear closely upon American national security, both in peace and war: strategies for fostering international cooperation with other states and nonstate actors; and a strategic information warfighting doctrine. We examine a variety of approaches to building robust coalition structures and consider the ways in which American influence can be advanced in a manner that

---

[2]This is the pronunciation we prefer, because it adheres best to the pronunciation of the Greek root *noos*. However, some dictionaries may indicate that other pronunciations are possible (e.g., n $\overline{o}$ -uh-poh-li-teek).

will neither threaten nor spark reactions. In the event that diplomatic strategy fails to prevent conflict, our view is that information weapons will have great effects upon the future "face of battle." With this in mind, we advance some doctrinal strategies that strive to reconcile the pragmatic need to strike powerfully with the ethical imperative to wage war justly.

Our study includes recommendations for policy, ranging from high-level emphasis on supporting the emergence of a global noosphere, to institutional recommendations that, for example, the U.S. military should begin to develop its own noosphere (among and between the services, as well as with U.S. friends and allies). In the area of international cooperation, we offer recommendations for strategic approaches to influence—but not alienate—the state and nonstate actors of the noosphere. Finally, we recommend specific doctrine related to information strategy—including the pressing need to deal with such ethical concerns as the first use of information weapons, concepts of proportional response, and the need to maintain, to the greatest extent possible, the immunity of noncombatants.

From these beginnings, we hope that an articulated, integrated, U.S. information strategy will emerge.

Chapter Two

RECOGNITION OF THE NOOSPHERE

WHY "INFORMATION" MATTERS

Information and communications have always been important to strategy. But they are moving from being subsidiary to becoming overarching concerns—"information" matters more than ever, for reasons that did not exist even 20 years ago.

One reason is technological innovation: the growth of a new information infrastructure that includes not only the Internet, but also cable systems, direct broadcast satellites, cellular phones, etc.—in which the balance is shifting from one-to-many broadcast media (e.g., traditional radio and television) to many-to-many interactive media. A huge increase in global interconnectivity is resulting from the ease of entry and access in many nations, and from the growing, though varied, interests of so many actors in using the new infrastructure for economic, social, diplomatic, military, and other interactions.

Thus, a second reason is the proliferation of new organizations: Vast new arrays of state and nonstate organizations are emerging that directly concern information and communications issues. The new organizational ecology is the richest in the United States, with such nongovernmental organizations (NGOs)[1] as the Electronic Freedom

---

[1]A word of clarification: NGOs are, for the most part, civil-society organizations. The point has been made to us several times by devotees of economic power that private, for-profit, commercial corporations are powerful NGOs. But this is incorrect usage. Such corporations are nonstate actors but are not NGOs—that term (and acronym)

Foundation (EFF) and Computer Professionals for Social Responsibility (CPSR) exemplifying the trend. These groups span the political spectrum and have objectives that range from helping people get connected to the Internet, to influencing government policies and laws, and advancing particular causes at home or abroad. It is not just the proliferation of such organizations, but also their interconnection in sprawling networks that makes them increasingly influential. As the strength of NGOs in particular and nonstate actors in general grows, the nature of world politics promises to become less state-centric.

A third reason is ideational: a spreading recognition that "information" and "power" are increasingly intertwined. Across all political, economic, and military areas, informational soft power (Nye, 1990; Nye and Owens, 1996) is becoming more important, compared to traditional hard power. This trend may take decades to unfold; in the interim, traditional methods of exercising power may remain squarely at the core of international politics. But meanwhile, the rise of soft power provides another reason for attending to the formulation of information strategy—power, security, and strategy are increasingly up for redefinition in the information age.

At all three levels—the technological, organizational, and ideational—"network effects" are taking hold, further helping explain why information is influencing more than ever people's behavior as well as government policies and strategies. Network effects mean, for example, that if only one person has a telephone or fax machine, it is not useful—he or she cannot communicate with anyone else. But as more people use phones and faxes, the value of each one increases, as does the value of the network as a whole.[2] According to "Metcalfe's law" (named after Robert Metcalfe, who designed the communication protocol governing the Ethernet), the "power" of a network is proportional to the square of the number of nodes in it.

---

apparently dates from the early years of the United Nations and was not meant to include commercial corporations. Neither was a related term, international nongovernmental organization (INGO), which we do not use here.

[2]The network effect involves not only expansion of a network but also standardization to ease access to it. Oft-cited stories about network effects explain, for example, why the VHS format prevailed over Beta in videocassette recorder technology, even though Beta was considered a superior technology.

Network effects may apply to the spread of not only new technologies, but also new organizations and ideas.

Together, these technological, organizational, and ideational developments mean that information is increasingly viewed as an agent of system change and transformation. They also mean that information-based realms are being created that thrive on network effects.

THREE CONCEPTS OF INFORMATION-BASED REALMS[3]

As information and communication have come to matter more, so have the realms or domains defined by them. The three that matter the most are cyberspace, the infosphere, and the noosphere.[4] All are about information, and all combine technological, organizational, and ideational elements. But each has a different focus and emphasis—and this affects their significance for strategy. They are discussed below in a progression, from the most technological (cyberspace), to the most ideational (the noosphere).

Analysts, strategists, and policymakers face choices as to which term(s) to prefer. The term *noosphere* may be difficult to adopt—it sounds weird. But recall that the term *cyberspace* was initially received this way—yet now it is routine. The term *infosphere* has never been so controversial; and, for many people, it may look like a good-enough term of art. However, it, like the other terms, has some inherent biases and limitations that should give pause, as noted below.

Meanwhile, some people may prefer to cast aside all three terms, in favor of just referring to a "realm of information," much as people

---

[3]Some of the writing in this section is repeated from Ronfeldt (1992).

[4]Dertouzos (1997) proposes another concept—the Information Marketplace—which means (p. 10)

> the collection of people, computers, communications, software, and services that will be engaged in the intraorganizational and interpersonal information transactions of the future.

In his view (p. 12), "the Information Marketplace—not Cyberspace—is the target toward which the Internet and the Web are headed." His concept is a variant of the infosphere, with an emphasis on economic motivations and transactions. But it has a noospheric element—he hopes for a coming "Age of Unification" in which the "techie-humie split" is resolved and a new agenda for humanism is served.

have long referred to the realms of politics, economics, and security. Eventually, that may make sense. However, in our view, it is too early to do that as a matter of course; the notion of a "realm of information" remains too overarching and all-inclusive, too shapeless and unbounded, to provide a sound basis for strategy. For the time being, it is more advisable to clarify and make better use of the concepts of cyberspace, the infosphere, and the noosphere.

Cyberspace

This, the most common of the three terms, refers to the global system of systems of internetted computers, communications infrastructures, online conferencing entities, databases, and information utilities generally known as the Net. This mostly means the Internet; but the term may also be used to refer to the specific, bounded electronic information environment of a corporation or of a military, government, or other organization.

The term serves to envision the electronic stocks and flows of information, the logged-in providers and users of that information, and the technologies linking them as a realm or system that has an identity as distinct as that of an economic or political system. Ideally, as technology advances, a user should be able to access and operate in cyberspace through hardware and software that render the impression of being inside a three-dimensional environment containing representations of the places, actors, instruments, and repositories that a user is interested in.

Cyberspace is the fastest growing, newest domain of power and property in the world. The Internet alone now embraces some 20 million computer hosts, nearly a hundred million users (expected to exceed a billion by the year 2000), and billions if not trillions of dollars' worth of activities. Further developing this realm, nationally and globally, is one of the great undertakings of our time. No wonder the term has gained such currency.

The term has a more technological bent than infosphere or noosphere. Yet, there has always been a tendency to see cyberspace as far more than technology, from the moment the term was proposed by cyberpunk writer William Gibson (1984) as a "consensual hallucination," through recent notions of cyberspace as a realm for building "virtual communities" (Rheingold, 1993), creating a "global matrix of minds" (Quarterman, 1990 and 1993), and strengthening people's spiritual bonds around the world (Cobb, 1998). Such views implicitly portend an overlap of cyberspace with the noosphere (see below).

Cyberspace is more bounded than the infosphere or the noosphere, in that it refers mainly to the Net. But some definitions extend beyond the Internet to include the public switched networks (PSNs) and other cyberspace access points and controls for affecting critical infrastructures: e.g., electric power grids, oil and gas pipelines, telecommunications systems, financial clearinghouses, air traffic control systems, railroad switching systems, truck location and dispatch systems, media broadcast systems, and military and other government security systems. Strategic information warfare is largely about assuring cyberspace security and safety at home, and developing a capacity to exploit vulnerabilities in systems abroad.

Infosphere

Knowing the spatial and technical limitations of the cyberspace concept, some analysts prefer the term *infosphere.* Sometimes the two terms are used interchangeably, or the distinctions between them are unclear. For example, in one recent view (Vlahos, 1998, p. 512),

> The Infosphere is shorthand for the fusion of all the world's communications networks, databases, and sources of information into a vast, intertwined and heterogeneous tapestry of electronic interchange. . . . The Infosphere has the potential to gather all people and all knowledge together into one place.

This could as easily be a definition of cyberspace in some quarters.

But, when defined distinctly, the infosphere is far larger than cyberspace—it encompasses the latter, plus a range of information systems that may not be part of the Net. In the civilian world, this often includes broadcast, print, and other media (i.e., the *mediasphere*), as well as institutions, such as public libraries, parts of which are not yet electronic. In the military world, the infosphere may include command, control, communications, intelligence, surveillance, and reconnaissance systems—the electronic systems of the "military information environment" (another term of art) above and around a battlespace.

According to Jeffrey Cooper (1997, pp. iii, 3, 27), the infosphere is emerging, like cyberspace, as a "truly global information infrastructure and environment" in which traditional notions of space and time no longer prevail. The term has merit because it focuses on "information environments," broadly defined, rather than on computerized technologies and infrastructures. The term is also favored because it "carries resonances of biosphere"—meaning that the infosphere is "a distinct domain built on information, but one intimately related to the rest of a set of nested globes in which we exist simultaneously."

In observing this, Jeffrey Cooper implicitly entertains a view of the world that partakes of the next concept. So does French philosopher Paul Virilio in the following insight from an interview with James der Derian (1996):

> I think that the infosphere—the sphere of information—is going to impose itself on the geosphere. We are going to be living in a reduced world. The capacity of interactivity is going to reduce the world to nearly nothing. In fact, there is already a speed pollution, which reduces the world to nothing. In the near future, people will feel enclosed in a small environment. They will have a feeling of confinement in the world, which will certainly be at the limit of tolerability, by virtue of the speed of information. If I were to offer you a last thought—interactivity is to real space what radioactivity is to the atmosphere.

Noosphere

The most abstract—and so far, least favored—of the available terms is that of the *noosphere.* This term, from the Greek word *noos* for "the mind," was coined by the controversial French theologian and scientist Pierre Teilhard de Chardin in 1925 and disseminated in posthumous publications in the 1950s and 1960s.[5] In his view, the

---

[5]Teilhard's belief in the need for an expansive, ethically based noosphere may have been based partly on his grim experiences during World War I, which are movingly chronicled in his correspondence from this period (Teilhard, 1961).

world first evolved a geosphere and next a biosphere. Now that people are communing on global scales, the world is giving rise to a noosphere—what he variously describes (1964 and 1965) as a globe-spanning realm of "the mind," a "thinking circuit," a "stupendous thinking machine," a "thinking envelope" full of fibers and networks, and a planetary "consciousness." In the words of Julian Huxley (in Teilhard, 1965, p. 18), the noosphere amounts to a "web of living thought."

According to Teilhard, forces of the mind have been creating and deploying pieces of the noosphere for ages. Now, it is finally achieving a global presence, and its varied "compartments" are fusing. Before long, a synthesis will occur in which peoples of different nations, races, and cultures will develop consciousness and mental activity that are planetary in scope, without losing their personal identities. Fully realized, the noosphere will raise mankind to a high, new evolutionary plane, one driven by a collective coordination of psychosocial and spiritual energies and by a devotion to moral and juridical principles. However, the transition may not be smooth; a global tremor and possibly an apocalypse may characterize the final fusion of the noosphere (1964, pp. 175–181; 1965, pp. 287–290).

Although this concept is essentially spiritual, and far less technological than cyberspace or the infosphere, Teilhard identified increased communications as a cause. Nothing like the Internet existed in his time. Yet 1950s-era radio and television systems were fostering the emergence of "a sort of 'etherized' universal consciousness," and he expected "astonishing electronic computers" to give mankind new tools for thinking (1964). Today, he is occasionally credited with anticipating the Internet. Indeed, the gestalt of *Wired* magazine evokes the creed that "an electronic membrane covering the earth would wire all humanity together in a single nervous system," giving rise to a global consciousness (from *Wired*, Vol. 6, No. 1, January 1998; also see Cobb, 1995). John Perry Barlow, a frequent *Wired* contributor and a cofounder of the Electronic Freedom Foundation, observes (in Cobb, 1998, p. 85) that

> [w]hat Teilhard was saying can be summed up in a few words. The point of all evolution to this stage is to create a collective organism of mind. With cyberspace, we are essentially hardwiring the noosphere.

Furthermore, Teilhard voiced, decades ago, many notions now in favor among information-age thinkers about complexity, the association of complexity with consciousness, and the shift from genes to what he called "noogenesis" (a vehicle for memes?[6]) as a basis of future human evolution.   His view of planetary society as a "superorganism" helped inspire Marshall McLuhan's notion of the "global village" and James Lovelock's and Lynn Margulis's "Gaia thesis" (which, in turn, influenced Vice President Albert Gore's ideas about keeping the Earth's environment in balance).

The noosphere concept thus encompasses cyberspace and the infosphere and has its own technological, organizational, and ideational levels. It relates to an organizational theme that has constantly figured in our own work about the information revolution: the rise of network forms of organization that strengthen civil-society actors (Arquilla and Ronfeldt, 1996a, 1997; Ronfeldt, 1996). Few state or market actors, by themselves, seem likely to have much interest in fostering the construction of a global noosphere, except in limited areas having to do with international law, or political and economic ideology. The impetus for creating a global noosphere is more likely to emanate from activist NGOs, other civil-society actors (e.g., churches and schools), and private individuals dedicated to freedom of information and communications and to the spread of ethical values and norms.[7]

Testimony for this comes from Elise Boulding, a scholar-activist who has long worked in peace networks. She sees, à la Teilhard, a "many-layered map of the world" consisting of the geosphere, biosphere, and what she calls the "sociosphere," which includes families, communities, nation-states, international organizations, and "the peoples' layer—the transnational network of international voluntary organizations" (Boulding, 1988, pp. 54–55). Atop that is the noosphere,

---

[6]Dawkins (1989) originated the notion of "memes" as a postgenetic basis for continued human evolution. Lynch (1996) discusses how memes may spread through "thought contagion."

[7]For a novel discussion that actually relies on the concept of the noosphere—arguing that open-source software is an expression of a gift-culture among hackers working in the noosphere, defined as "the territory of ideas, the space of all possible thoughts"—see Eric S. Raymond, *Homesteading the Noosphere*, April 1998, posted at http://www.tuxedo.org/~esr/writings/.

which consists of "the sum total of all the thoughts generated in the sociosphere." In her view,

> [t]he more we can involve ourselves in the networks that give us access to that envelope, the more we can contribute to the emergence of that [global civic] culture.

Her hope is that globe-circling associations of private citizens will foster a "global civic culture" based on the notion that people of various nationalities have common interests. NGOs and other groupings of ethically minded individuals, energized by a noospheric culture, could alter how the world is governed (Boulding, 1988 and 1993).

Boulding's writings, in addition to others' (e.g., Frederick, 1993a and b), indicate that the noosphere concept has gained more resonance and credibility among transnational civil-society actors than among government and commercial actors. We believe it is time for the latter to begin moving in this direction, too, particularly since power in the information age will stem, more than ever before, from the ability of state and market actors to work conjointly with civil-society actors.

COMPARISONS LEAD TO A PREFERENCE FOR THE NOOSPHERE CONCEPT

All three realms are under development and will remain so. Even though all are expanding rapidly around the world, they are still split into compartments, which are more advanced in some parts of the world than in others. A steady internetting of their varied compartments is under way (although a total worldwide fusion seems unlikely, if only because of some actors' interests in protecting partitions in some areas). But even as the three realms grow, they will continue to overlap. Cyberspace will remain the smallest, nested inside the other two. The infosphere is the next largest, and the noosphere encompasses all three (see the Figure). As one realm grows, so should the others—although not necessarily evenly.

None of the three concepts should be dismissed—all are useful. But their biases should be recognized. The realms all have technological,

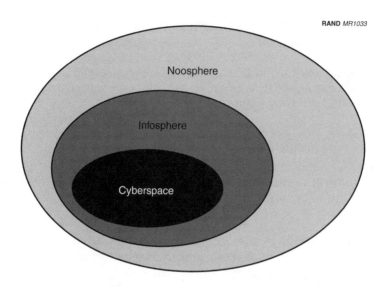

RAND *MR1033*

Figure—Three Realms of Information

organizational, and ideational levels; but these levels, and their significance, are somewhat different for each. Moreover, each has an
inherent image that may affect how a person thinks about each.[8] Of
the three, the core image for cyberspace is the most technological,
the noosphere the most idealized.   When a person thinks
"cyberspace," what typically comes to mind is a computer screen
logged onto the Internet—whether the content on the screen is civilized or uncivilized is beside the point.   When a person thinks
"infosphere," the image is likely a television showing something
along the lines of a CNN broadcast conveyed by a satellite. When a
person thinks of the "noosphere," the image will not be of a technology, but probably of an idea floating in a cultural ether—and the
content is likely civilized.

While discussions about the expansion of cyberspace tend to be
technological, discussions about the infosphere often emphasize
commercial motivations and considerations. In contrast, discussions

---

[8]On the roles of metaphors in thinking, see Lakoff and Johnson (1980).

about the future of the noosphere, although they remain few and far between, are bound to be philosophical. Table 1 lays out some of the ideational, organizational, and technological aspects of each of the realms.

Of course, whichever realm serves as the point of departure, discussions of issues may well branch in the direction of another realm. Thus, many a discussion of cyberspace may turn rather noospheric. For example, military analysts who talk about information warfare waged via cyberspace or the infosphere may argue that such warfare is really about people's mentalities, and about attacking their perceptions and epistemologies (see Szafranski, 1994 and 1995; Stein, 1995). While there has been much discussion about hackers taking down the Net, it is also the case that U.S. perceptions may be "hacked" by adversaries and manipulators who want the Net up, so they can air their pronouncements in the broadcast media as well as on the Internet (see Toffler and Toffler, 1993; De Caro, 1996; Libicki, 1997). At the same time, information-age philosophers (e.g., Cobb, 1995 and 1998) who favor the noosphere concept note that its growth depends on the worldwide proliferation of highly accessible, internetted information and communications systems.

But the point remains—the noosphere is the most ideational realm. In so being, it has a comparative strength. Cyberspace, the infosphere, and the noosphere are realms based on "information" in all its guises, from lowly bits of data to the highest forms of knowledge and wisdom. Thus these realms are all information-processing systems. Yet, in being more about ideas than technologies, the noosphere, more than the other realms, also concerns "information

Table 1

Information Realms Across Three Levels

	Cyberspace	Infosphere	Noosphere
Ideational tenets	Interconnectivity and democracy	Prosperity and interdependence	Sharing ideas
Organizational exemplars	Internet Society, EFF, CPSR	CNN, Disney, Time-Warner	Peace NGOs, universities, the UN
Technological conduits	Internet, the Web	Radio, TV, cable	Educational and training systems

structuring." The noosphere, like the mind, is an information-processing and an information-structuring system—and this is an important distinction. The processing view focuses on the transmission of messages as the inputs and outputs of a system. In contrast, the structural view illuminates the goals, values, and practices[9] that an organization or system embodies—what matters to its members from the standpoint of identity, meaning, and purpose, apart from whether any information is being processed at the time (see Arquilla and Ronfeldt, 1997 and 1998a). While the processing view tends to illuminate technology as a critical factor, the structural view is more likely to uphold human and ideational capital.

In our view, strategists should begin attending as much to the dynamics of information structuring as to information processing. Grand strategists rarely ignore the role of values and practices. But lately this role tends to be downplayed in rhetoric about the information revolution. We believe that new concepts can provide a corrective. Adoption of the noosphere concept could help information strategists focus on the significance of information structuring.

Comparatively, all three realms raise similar propositions about the long-range future of human society. These propositions entail similar hopes and fears, ambiguities and paradoxes. Consider, as one example, the following McLuhanesque observation, which heralds the emergence of a "global village"—but could equally be about cyberspace, the infosphere, or noosphere. Similar remarks have been made, repeatedly, about each of these realms:

> Electric circuitry has overthrown the regime of "time" and "space" and pours upon us instantly and continuously concerns of all other men. It has reconstituted dialogue on a global scale. Its message is

---

[9]Compared to traditional concepts like ends, values, and norms, "practices" is a recent addition in the literature on social thought and behavior. For example, Bellah et al. (1996) state that

> Practices are shared activities that are not undertaken as means to an end but are ethically good in themselves (thus close to *praxis* in Aristotle's sense). A genuine community—whether a marriage, a university, or a whole society—is constituted by such practices.

This concept goes to the heart of what is meant by "structural information." We are grateful to George Denning for pointing out the concept of practices and its relevance for thinking about structural information.

Total Change, ending psychic, social, economic, and political parochialism. . . . Ours is a brand-new world of allatonceness. "Time" has ceased, "space" has vanished. We now live in a global village . . . a simultaneous happening (McLuhan, Fiore, and Agel, 1967, pp. 16 and 63).

If one accepts the spatial and temporal shifts as McLuhan lauds them, then a united, global village is in the making. Yet, that is not the only possible implication. Like Teilhard and McLuhan, Daniel Bell (1977, pp. 26–27) foresaw, years prior to the Internet, that technology is resulting in "the eclipse of distance and the foreshortening of time, almost to the fusion of the two." But in his view, instability and insecurity were likely implications. Societies, the United States in particular, are undergoing a "loss of insulating space" as conditions and events in one place are quickly, demandingly, transmitted to other places. Political systems are becoming more permeable to destabilizing events, and people are more able to respond directly and immediately. In some societies—Bell was mainly worried about the United States—this raises the likelihood not of a vital community but of contagious mass reactions and mobilizations that may allow rulers to tighten their grip.[10]

In sum, the information revolution contributes to both the integration and the fragmentation occurring around the world today. This is evident via all three realms—cyberspace, the infosphere, and the noosphere—although the last may be the best suited to illuminate value-laden conflicts.

Against this background, should any of the three concepts—cyberspace, the infosphere, or the noosphere—be preferred by information strategists? To date, strategists have worked mostly in terms of the first two. Our recommendation is that they turn to work equally if not mainly in terms of the third. This is not to say that all

---

[10]One way for leaders and their regimes to tighten their grip on society and its potential malcontents and malefactors is by using the new information realms for surveillance. For a recent discussion, see a study known as the Scientific and Technological Options (STOA) Interim Study, "An Appraisal of the Technologies of Political Control," Executive Summary, prepared by Steve Wright (Manchester Group) for the European Parliament, September 1998, as available on the Internet. This study provides an overview of high-tech surveillance innovations occurring in Europe and elsewhere around the world.

who read our report should rush to peruse Teilhard's writings; his views, though inspiring, remain unclear and abstruse.[11] Nonetheless, the noosphere concept has appealing features: Little is lost analytically and much may be gained by focusing equally on the noosphere as on the other two realms. It is the broadest of the three—and broader tends to mean better for strategic thinking and planning. The noosphere presents information in terms of an expanding realm where the emphasis is on the ideational and organizational dimensions, without ignoring the technological one. It inclines the analyst and the strategist to think in terms of the roles of ideas, values, and norms, rather than in terms of Internet hosts, Web sites, and baud rates—that is, in terms of structural information rather than in terms of information processing. More to our point, preferring the noosphere concept sets the stage for a key thesis of this study: The time is ripening to develop a new approach to grand strategy, one we call *noopolitik* and describe more fully in the next chapter.

EMERGENCE AND CONSTRUCTION OF THE NOOSPHERE

Figuring out the noosphere will require years of prodigious analysis. The structures and processes that are shaping its emergence will surely be no simpler than has been the case with the geosphere, biosphere, and sociosphere. And fully developed, the noosphere will surely be an enormous, complex realm of activity that, like the other spheres, has its own dynamics. Even so, aspects of its nature may be molded, at least in part, by determined actors operating inside it, and by what happens outside it, especially in the sociosphere. Thus, as the noosphere emerges on its own, in ways not easy to analyze, it may also, to some extent, be responsive to deliberate efforts at design and construction.

Take another look at the Figure and Table 1. The United States, in all its fullness and variety, is the world's leader in the creation—and construction—of cyberspace and the infosphere. The United States

---

[11]Readers who want to learn more about Teilhard's ideas, without struggling through his writings, can find sympathetic overviews in Wright (1989, pp. 258–274) and Cobb (1998). There are also many valuable writings—for example, in parts of Bateson (1972), Capra (1996), Castells (1996, 1997), and Dertouzos (1997)—that contain expositions about the rise of forces of the mind around the world, but without explicitly discussing Teilhard or the concept of the noosphere.

as a whole, much less the U.S. government, does not and cannot control these globe-girdling realms. But control is not the point. These realms have grown so much—and Americans are benefiting more than anyone else—because the United States has a constellation of values (like freedom and innovation), interests, actors, and technological capabilities that is bound to stimulate such growth. Moreover, the genius inherent in this constellation seems less about control than about a capacity for political and economic *decontrol*[12] that is unmatched elsewhere in the world when it comes to creating and building such realms of information.

America stands on the brink of a similar, but tougher, situation with regard to the noosphere. There is a good prospect, but a limited one with no guarantee, that American ideas, agents, and practices may govern much of its content and the conduct it inspires. Yet, the noosphere's emergence derives from myriad—not just American—forces around the world. There must be room for peoples and traditions that are different from America's, as well as room for such newly empowered nonstate actors as global civil-society NGOs that may care little about national identity and sovereignty. Also, the noosphere must contain an ethical brightness and solidity—but here again there is a risky downside: Such "uncivil society" actors as terrorists and criminals may be able to exploit aspects of it, or at least of its conduits, for their own dark purposes. Moreover, unless solidly articulated, a noosphere may be distorted by new "isms" (e.g., based on religious revivalism, or ethnonationalism) that appeal to people who may feel left out.

Thus, the emergence and construction of the noosphere is unlikely to be smooth, easily guidable, or uniformly positive in its effects. Since its design will rest on a complex bundle of ideational, organizational, and technological elements, it may give rise to unusual, unexpected dynamics. Perhaps, like other complex systems, it will sometimes surprise people with intimidating turbulence, "normal accidents"

---

[12]For a discussion about how being "out of control" can benefit a system, see Kelly (1994).

(à la Perrow, 1984),[13] and unintended consequences (see Tenner, 1996; Jervis, 1997) that could prove unpleasant for Americans.

Despite these potential difficulties, it behooves Americans to make an effort to foster the rise of the noosphere, in harmony with American ideals and interests. The policy choices involve the extent to which, and how, the noosphere's pending emergence can be shaped through deliberate actions. All public, private, state, and nonstate sectors of U.S society could play roles; the U.S. government could play a substantial role.

But the following conundrum should be thought through. States can assist with the construction of a noosphere, for example, through policies that assure openness, information sharing, and the rule of law. Yet, the noosphere cannot be an artifact of states, much less the instrument of any single state. Indeed, a true noosphere, given its global nature, may serve to restrict some state actions—and not only aggressive, inhumane ones. In subtle ways not yet apparent, even states that behave justly may find themselves more constrained than in the heyday of the state. There is some evidence, for example, that the "CNN effect" of showing horrendous images of human suffering from places like Bosnia and Rwanda—in short, images provided by the noosphere—helped prompt U.S. involvements in areas far removed from its recognized spheres of interest. Further, a fully functioning noosphere may, under some circumstances, make it more difficult to use legitimate military force against an actor whom a state wants to stop (e.g., a Saddam Hussein). Does this mean, paradoxically, that the U.S. government would risk undoing its own power and presence if it undertook to encourage a noosphere? Perhaps—if it were to use its power and presence in state-centric, unilateral terms. Yet not at all—to reiterate a point made throughout this study—if it learns to work conjointly with nonstate (and other state) actors to bring off the formation of a global noosphere. This is an undertaking for multiactor networks, not stand-alone hierarchies.

What would a full-fledged noosphere encompass? What ideas, values, and norms—what principles, practices, and rules—should it

---

[13]Perrow (1984) shows that occasional, even catastrophic, accidents may be a normal feature of high-tech high-risk systems whose parts are tightly rather than loosely coupled, and whose interactions are complex (nonlinear) rather than linear.

embody? We presume that these would include much that America stands for: openness, freedom, democracy, the rule of law, humane behavior, respect for human rights, a preference for peaceful conflict resolution, etc. The growth of the noosphere will depend not only on increased *flows* of ideas and ideals, but also on growth in the *stocks* of ideas and ideals to which people subscribe. In addition, a noosphere may have to have complex organizational and technological bases to support its ideational essence.

Going into these matters in detail is more than this preliminary study can accomplish. But openness, progress, and knowledge are briefly discussed below, the first because it is so essential to a noosphere, the second and third because they are not so obvious but may prove to be essential over the long run.

Openness is utterly essential for a global noosphere. It cannot come into being or endure without openness, along with a commitment to the cohorts of openness—freedom and democracy. Openness is not merely an American philosophical abstraction. Various policy analysts (e.g., see Shultz, 1985) have shown that the information revolution serves to open up closed systems, and that only open systems can take full advantage of the new forms of power it generates. Indeed, the spread of democracy is related to the spread of connectivity (Kedzie, 1997). In addition, the new technologies, along with a commitment to deeply share information, could make the world impeccably transparent, perhaps along the lines that David Brin (1998) calls "reciprocal transparency"—which seems quite appropriate for a noosphere.[14]

A full-fledged noosphere should embody some concepts of what constitutes "progress" for humanity. At present, this is a contentious matter. The end of the Cold War inspired a conviction that liberal democratic societies with strong market systems and civil societies were best, having won the evolutionary competition. But lately, in many parts of the world, debates are growing anew as to whether America's, or any other society's, model of progress is commendable

---

[14]This is not to deny the importance of informational guardedness, as in our notion of "guarded openness" discussed later in this report. Indeed, in some areas guardedness may well serve to protect openness. But openness, not guardedness per se, is the essential requisite for the creation and construction of a noosphere.

for all. "Illiberal democracy" (see Zakaria, 1997) has even come into vogue as a transitional model. Moreover, postmodernist thinking among Western intellectuals is currently fond of raising doubts about whether progress truly exists as a definable ideal, free of ethnocentric, religious, or other presumptions. Such negativism and relativism will not likely serve the rise of a noosphere. The noosphere begs for a positive *telos* or goal—not so much that it would be vulnerable to charges of being irredeemably teleological, but enough to link it to serving high ends. Just what may be the best concept of progress—or the right theory of societal evolution—for a noosphere? It remains unclear, but we presume that the noosphere should prefer democratic system change, although it may accept, within limits, whatever system a particular people may choose to suit their circumstances. Complete accord about the meaning and nature of progress may be asking too much; but a better, more harmonious consensus is needed than exists today.[15] A noosphere will have difficulty emerging if a "clash of civilizations" (à la Huntington, 1996) prevails in sections of the world.

A noosphere is a realm of knowledge and wisdom. The very concept implies that some kinds of knowledge will, and should, prevail over other kinds—that there is agreement as to the nature and sources of true knowledge. Thus the concept may seem to imply an integration across all branches of learning—"consilience," to use the term proposed by biologist E. O. Wilson (1998). But it need not mean that. Scientific knowledge may eventually be subject to consilience, but knowledge that stems from culture (not to mention countercultures and subcultures) is another matter. In the words of anthropologist Peter Worsley (1997, p. 10), "Knowledge, then, is necessarily plural: there are knowledges, not simply Knowledge with a capital K." If a noosphere is to appeal to people all around the world, it must allow for a diversity of knowledge, much as a large ecosystem with diverse plant life may prove healthier than an ecosystem where diversity is stymied.

Without depth and breadth in such areas, a noosphere is unlikely to serve as a strong, globe-circling reference for all peoples and soci-

---

[15]Writings by Sanderson (1995) and by Ronfeldt (1996) may provide instructive insights for working out a theory of societal evolution that is consistent with the emergence of a noosphere.

eties, with a capacity not only to guide behavior in positive, inclusive ways, but also to tamp down unjust, exclusivist ideas. Keen challenges for the construction of a noosphere may stem from the fact that the new technologies enable all manner of information-age actors to project their presence into distant locations where they may infringe on local traditions and priorities. These actors range from the satellite broadcast companies of such leaders as Rupert Murdoch and Ted Turner, to the expatriate dissidents who want to reach into their homelands in China, Cuba, Saudi Arabia, and elsewhere. This augurs for mighty struggles to dominate the Internet, satellite broadcasting, and other media as part and parcel of the formation of a global noosphere.

Chapter Three

EMERGENCE OF NOOPOLITIK

GRAND STRATEGIC SHIFTS AT THE TURN OF THE CENTURY

The end of the Cold War has brought two major shifts that appeal to grand strategists. The first concerns political and military dynamics. The bipolar international system has expired, and the world appears to be returning to a loose, multipolar, balance-of-power system, with possibilities for U.S. dominance in key military areas. Since this shift is largely about interstate relations, it arouses the theorists and practitioners of realpolitik. The second shift is mainly economic: the enormous growth of liberal market systems woven together in global trade and investment webs. This shift began long before the Cold War ended and is now ascendant. Its dynamics appeal especially to the liberal-internationalist or global-interdependence schools of strategy, whose proponents argue, contrary to realists and neorealists, that statist dynamics matter less than in the past, and that the prospects for peace depend on multilateral cooperation through international regimes that transcend the state.

The result of these shifts is not only a changing world, but also a continuing interplay between America's two main schools of grand strategy: realpolitik and liberal internationalism.[1] Meanwhile, a

---

[1]Informative manifestations of this appear in the Spring 1998 issue of *Foreign Policy*, whose cover theme is "Frontiers of Knowledge: The State of the Art in World Affairs," and in the Autumn 1998 issue of *International Organization*, whose theme is "Exploration and Contestation in the Study of World Politics." While these (and other) journals emphasize the interplay between the *academic* schools of realism and

third, emerging shift has been noted: the intensification of the information revolution, with its implications that knowledge is power,
that power is diffusing to nonstate actors, and that global interconnectivity is generating a new fabric for world order. Many theorists
and strategists do not seem to know quite what to do with this shift.
Some view it as spelling a paradigm change, but most still try to make
it fit into either of the paramount paradigms about realpolitik and
internationalism.

Here we reassess how the information age is affecting the two dominant paradigms and call for a new paradigm for U.S. strategy. The
structures and dynamics of world order are changing so deeply that
neither realpolitik nor internationalism suits the new realities of the
information age well enough. A new paradigm is needed—in fact, it
is already emerging, especially in nongovernmental circles consisting
of civil society actors—which we call noopolitik.[2] The term extends
from our finding in the prior chapter that a global noosphere is taking shape—the development of cyberspace, the infosphere, and the
noosphere make noopolitik possible, and information strategy will
be its essence.

FROM REALPOLITIK TO NOOPOLITIK—A COMPARISON OF THE PARADIGMS

Noopolitik makes sense because knowledge is fast becoming an ever
stronger source of power and strategy, in ways that classic realpolitik

---

liberalism, they have also, in just the past few years, begun addressing the emergence
of a third school known as constructivism (or social constructivism). It holds that
ideational factors—e.g., social identities, and norms—determine the nature of
international reality, as much as do material factors. Thus, the concepts behind
constructivism are much like those behind our notion of noopolitik. However, we do
not discuss constructivism in this study, mainly because, unlike realism and liberal
internationalism, this new academic school does not yet figure in the worlds of policy
analysis. For good overviews of constructivism, see Ruggie (1998), and Hopf (1998).

[2]In our view, other possible terms like *cyberpolitik* or *infopolitik* are not appealing.
We considered and rejected the term cyberpolitik, because we wanted to focus attention on the noosphere, not cyberspace, and because we wanted a term whose connotation would be less technological and more ideational, which is in keeping with the
noosphere concept. Also, we felt that yet another term with a *cyber* prefix would not
take hold. However, see Rothkopf (1998, p. 326) for an illumination of why "the *realpolitik* of the new era is *cyberpolitik*, in which the actors are no longer just states,
and raw power can be countered or fortified by information power."

and internationalism cannot absorb. Noopolitik is an approach to statecraft, to be undertaken as much by nonstate as by state actors, that emphasizes the role of soft power in expressing ideas, values, norms, and ethics through all manner of media. This makes it distinct from realpolitik, which stresses the hard, material dimensions of power and treats states as the determinants of world order. Noopolitik has much in common with internationalism, but we would argue that the latter is a transitional paradigm that can be folded into noopolitik.

In the coming years, grand strategists interested in information strategy will be drawn to both realpolitik and noopolitik. As noopolitik takes shape and gains adherents, it will serve sometimes as a supplement and complement to realpolitik, and sometimes as a contrasting, rival paradigm for policy and strategy. As time passes and the global noosphere swells, noopolitik may provide a more relevant paradigm than realpolitik.

Looming Limitations of Realpolitik

Realpolitik may be defined as a foreign-policy behavior based on state-centered calculations of raw power and the national interest, guided by a conviction that might makes right (see Kissinger, 1994). Classic realpolitik—as put into practice by Cardinal Richelieu, Prince Metternich, and Otto von Bismarck—depends on *raison d'etat*, whereby "reasons of state" (including maximizing the state's freedom of action) take precedence over individual rights. It advances state interests by aiming to create and preserve a balance of power that keeps any state from becoming hegemonic or otherwise too powerful, in the expectation that balancing behavior by all parties can produce a self-regulating equilibrium. In a multipolar environment, realpolitik regards balancing acts as the essence of strategy, the way to keep order and avoid chaos (see Waltz, 1979). And it requires that alliances and other balancing acts be based strictly on power calculations, with little regard for whether an ally has similar or different beliefs—a major power should seek alliances that restrain a rival, even if "moral compromises and odious associations" are necessary at times.[3] In this light, realpolitik tends to be amoral. But it works best at constraining adversarial behavior if the players share some common values (see Morgenthau, 1948; Kissinger, 1994). Since it is state-centric, it admits only a grudging, selective recognition of nonstate actors.

Although realpolitik has been the dominant paradigm of statecraft for several centuries, it should not be taken for granted as a permanent paradigm. It emerged in a particular epoch in Europe, when the nation-state was gaining strength as the key form of societal organization, ending another epoch when the aspiration was to integrate all Europe under a Holy Roman Empire blessed by the Catholic Church (Kissinger, 1994). Thus, realpolitik spelled a harsh departure from the then-prevailing paradigm for diplomacy, which called for building a universal empire, not a competitive system of nation-states; which was rationalized by moral law, not raw power calculations; and which often worked more through marriage politics than power politics, as dynasties and aristocratic clans used intermarriages to extend their sway.[4] Although it is identified with the academic school known as realism, it should also be noted that realpolitik has no corner on the notion of being realistic. All these approaches to strategy—from marriage diplomacy to realpolitik, and noopolitik— amount to different ways of being realistic by making sensible, appropriate cost-benefit, win-loss, and risk calculations, as suited to the realities of the times.

Realpolitik retains a strong hold on statecraft today, but once again the world is entering a new epoch, and there are many signs that realpolitik is reaching its limits as a reflection of underlying realities. Realpolitik works best where states fully rule the international system—but nonstate actors from the worlds of commerce and civil society are gaining strength and reshaping the international environment. It works best where states can maneuver freely and independently—but complex transnational interconnections increasingly

---

[3]Phrase from Huntington, 1991, p. 16.

[4]This progression—from marriage politics to realpolitik, to noopolitik—appears to reflect a progression in the evolution of societies (discussed in Ronfeldt, 1996), from those centered first around the rise of tribes and clans, then around hierarchical institutions, and later markets, with networks now on the rise as the next great form of social organization.

constrain this. It works best where national interests dominate decisionmaking—but a host of "global issues" is arising that transcends national interests. It works best where states respond mainly to coercive calculations and applications of hard power—but state and nonstate actors are increasingly operating in terms of soft power. It works best where ethics matter little—but ethics are increasingly coming to the fore as global civil-society actors gain voice through all types of media. It works best where there is no such thing as a globe-circling noosphere to take into account—but one is emerging. Furthermore, realpolitik works best where diplomacy and strategy can be conducted mainly in the dark, away from public scrutiny, under strong state control, and without necessarily having to share information with many actors—but the information revolution is making all that increasingly difficult and is favoring actors who can operate in the light and gain advantage from information sharing. Indeed, the information revolution underlies most of the transformations noted above—it is the information revolution, above all else, that is delimiting the appropriateness of realpolitik.

Realpolitik has a natural reaction to the information revolution: It inclines strategists to prefer state control of informational stocks and flows, and to stress guardedness over openness when it comes to issues of sharing with others (unless there is a clear cost-benefit advantage to being open). A realpolitik posture is evident, for example, in governmental efforts to impose legal and technical controls over encryption. This resembles realpolitik's past mercantilist treatment of commerce.

Realpolitik can be modified and adapted to the information revolution, so that it remains an active paradigm.[5] Indeed, the international political system may be returning to a condition of loose multipolarity; and state-centric balance-of-power games will surely remain crucial at times and in places (e.g., in the Middle East and Asia). But seeking favorable balances of power in a multipolar system is only one process that U.S. strategy should take into

---

[5]Maynes (1997) discusses the prospects for "ethical realpolitik." Rothkopf (1998) aims to modify realpolitik under the rubric of cyberpolitik and analyzes how the information revolution is altering the traditional political, economic, and military pillars of U.S. policy and strategy—but his essay is less clear as to what cyberpolitik may actually consist of in the future.

account. Global interdependence (and interconnection), combined with the prospect that the United States is becoming a global power, as distinct from a national one, suggests that no ordinary balance-of-power game-of-nations lies ahead—American information strategists will need more than realpolitik in their tool kits.

Liberal Internationalism—A Transitional Paradigm

Liberal internationalism (or global interdependence)—the principal paradigm that has aspired to moderate if not supersede realpolitik—also does not provide an adequate basis for American information strategy. A more recent paradigm, since it requires high levels of economic transactions that did not exist when realpolitik emerged, internationalism has roots that lie in 19th century liberal views that held that increases in trade openness would foster harmonious, prosperous interdependence among nations, and that economic interdependence would make war unthinkable. This view was first elucidated in the 19th century "Manchester Creed,"[6] and then extolled by Sir Norman Angell (1913), who declared war "dead" because of the peace-enhancing properties of interlocking trade and the unacceptable costs of conflict. Ironically, World War I broke out soon after publication of his ideas. Furthermore, this paradigm—under the rubric of "Wilsonian internationalism" (named for U.S. President Woodrow Wilson)—aspired to replace raw power calculations with an understanding that the spread of democratic values, and their enshrinement in international institutions, would prevent conflict, in part by encouraging ever greater economic interdependence and openness.

The seminal academic writings about "complex global interdependence" by Robert Keohane and Joseph Nye (1972 and 1977) fleshed out this paradigm, showing that the state-centric balance-of-power paradigm neglects the growing influence of transnational ties. Indeed, the trends heralded two decades ago by the prognosticators of interdependence are still unfolding: the global diffusion of power, the erosion of both national sovereignty and international hierarchy,

---

[6]The Manchester Creed epitomized 19th century classical liberal thought, positing the notion that free markets and expanded trade would leave little or no room for warmaking.

the growth of transnational economics and communications, the internationalization of domestic policy, the blurring and the fusion of domestic and foreign policy, the rise of multilateral diplomacy, and the need to broaden security concepts beyond their military dimensions (from Nye, 1976). Recently, interdependence theory has been revivified by a notion that states are becoming "trading states" who see no profit in war—and thus have no reason to go to war (see Rosecrance, 1984).

In general terms, the interdependence paradigm furthers the Wilsonian quest to create state-based global regimes to regulate and resolve specific issues. However, the goal is not simply to build new bureaucratic hierarchies that stand above states, but rather to embed states in a set of constraining transnational networks:

> The international organization model assumes that a set of networks, norms, and institutions, once established, will be difficult either to eradicate or drastically to rearrange. Even governments with superior capabilities—overall or within the issue area—will find it hard to work their will when it conflicts with established patterns of behavior within existing networks and institutions (Keohane and Nye, 1977, p. 55).

Meanwhile, a key notion that interdependence will tamp down conflict and ensure peace has not fared well—even though the record is mixed, the world remains as turbulent as ever, if not more so. This has left the door open for critics to reiterate the realpolitik mantra: Statecraft based on realpolitik may not be any better at preventing conflict, but at least power balancing can restore an equilibrium once it has been disturbed. Indeed, the interdependence paradigm has been subjected to constant heavy criticism by realists and neorealists who argue that, on all essential matters, states continue to rule the international system, and that international regimes of any influence merely reflect this (see Mearsheimer, 1994–1995; Waltz, 1979). Moreover, a case can be made that the structures and dynamics of the world economy reflect economic multipolarity (i.e., realpolitik) as much as economic interdependence.

Nonetheless, the internationalism paradigm keeps pace with the new realities of the information age better than realpolitik does. But even so, it too has some notable weaknesses and shortcomings. Although it effectively emphasizes the spread of transnational ties, it does so mainly in economic terms, despite some nods to increased information and communication flows. And although it recognizes the growth in influence of actors besides states, including NGOs, it mainly spotlights multinational corporations and international organizations composed of state representatives, while barely keeping up with the growth in influence of global civil-society NGOs. Lastly, although it heralds the rise of network forms of organization, it takes more a top-down than a bottom-up approach to them.

Not long ago, a leading proponent of the interdependence paradigm has responded to the information revolution with a major contribution: the concept of soft power (Nye, 1990; Nye and Owens, 1996). As noted earlier, this concept relates to the idea-sharing pole of information strategy, which is most in need of development. The soft power approach contravenes realpolitik's emphasis on raw power. It also contravenes realpolitik's inherently guarded orientation toward the information revolution, by favoring postures of openness and sharing with allies and other actors. Moreover, even where guardedness is needed, soft power allows for less-pronounced statist options than does realpolitik—for example, in relation to freedom of encryption.

Much of liberal internationalism is so close in spirit and substance to noopolitik that, with modification, it may be absorbed by it. A line runs from Wilsonian internationalism, through interdependence theory, to noopolitik, although it is more a broken than a straight line.

NOOPOLITIK IN THEORY AND PRACTICE

An old metaphor about realpolitik views world politics in Newtonian terms as though states, as the only important game pieces, were the only billiard balls moving around on a pool table. What would be more accurate now is a post-Newtonian metaphor, or at least a changed understanding of this old one. The new metaphor should not only add balls for nonstate actors, but should also show that what happens on the table depends on the dynamics of the table fabric as well as the interactions among the balls. And, metaphorically speaking, that fabric is changing in ways that make it—the fabric itself—a new and important factor.[7]

Trends That Invite Noopolitik

Noopolitik makes sense because trends exist that make it increasingly viable. We identify five trends: the growing fabric of global interconnection, the continued strengthening of global civil society, the rise of soft power, the new importance of "cooperative advantages," and the formation of the global noosphere. These trends do not spell the obsolescence of realpolitik, but they are at odds with it. To a lesser degree, they are also at odds with the tenets of liberal internationalism. We discuss each of the five trends below.

Global Interconnection. The era of global interdependence began in the 1960s, and many trends its theorists emphasize continue to come true. However, the term "interdependence" is wearing, and is not quite right for our purposes. It retains a primarily economic connotation; it is overly associated with recommendations for the creation of state-based international regimes; and it connotes the rather traditional, even negative, dynamics of "dependence," as in the contrast between independence and interdependence. Moreover, the term does not quite convey the point we want to make—that a new "fabric" of relations is emerging in the information age, weaving the world and all its key actors together. In our view, the coming age is defined better by the term "interconnection." America and Americans are moving out of the age of global interdependence into one of global interconnection.

There are many reasons why the world became interdependent, and changes in those reasons help explain why interconnection may be the best word to describe the situation. These include the following: a shift in the underlying nature of interdependence, the global rise of nonstate actors, and the emergence of global networks of interest and activity.

---

[7]We were inspired to pose this metaphorical reference after a meeting of the Highlands Forum in November 1997, where several attendees broached the obsolescence of the billiard-balls metaphor in a discussion about diplomacy in the information age. Theoretical writings about complexity also sometimes raise this kind of metaphor.

First, the world became interdependent because transnational "flows" of all kinds—capital, labor, technology, information, etc.—became immense. But as the flows have grown, the "stocks" that receiving nations accumulate from the sending nations—e.g., foreign immigration and investment—have grown large and permanent. For many nations, the nature of interdependence is now defined not only by the flows, but increasingly by the presence of foreign stocks that are self-perpetuating, and that have multiple, complex economic, cultural, and other local consequences.[8] Thus, societies are becoming connected in new ways.

This change combines with a second: Interdependence was spurred by the rise of transnational and multinational actors, especially multinational corporations and multilateral organizations. Now, a new generation of actors—e.g., news media, electronic communications services, human-rights organizations—are increasingly "going global," some to the point of claiming they are "stateless" and denying they are "national" or "multinational" in character. They are redefining themselves as global actors with global agendas, and pursuing global expansion through ties with like-minded counterparts. Interconnection impels this expansion.

Third, the capital, technology, information, and other flows that have moved the world down the interdependence path were initially quite inchoate, episodic, and disconnected from each other. That is no longer the case—the best example being that a global financial system has taken shape. These new flows and stocks are resulting in myriad, seamless networks of economic, social, and other relationships. As these become institutionalized, state and nonstate actors acquire interests in the growth of these networks separate from the national and local interests they may have. This growth requires continued interconnection. For some global actors, building and protecting the new networks become more important than building and protecting national power balances—as the networks themselves become sources of power for their members.

Some global actors are thus looking at the world more in terms of widespread networks than in terms of distinct groups and nations lo-

---

[8]These points about stocks and flows are repeated from Ronfeldt and Ortíz de Oppermann (1990, Ch. 6).

cated in specific places. The process of global interconnection is concentrated among the industrialized nations of the Northern Hemisphere. Yet, the growth of the global "borderless" economy often means that the key beneficiaries are not nations per se but particular subregions, such as Alsace-Lorraine, Wales, Kansai, Orange County (see Ohmae, 1990, 1995), as well as "world cities" (e.g., London, Los Angeles, and Tokyo) that are becoming so linked as to represent collectively a distributed "global city" (Brand, 1989; Sassen, 1991; Kotkin; 1993). The United States is increasingly a global, as distinct from a purely national, actor.

In sum, interconnecting the world may be the most forward-looking "game" in the decades ahead—as or more important than the balance-of-power game. Barring a reversion to anarchy or other steps backward—e.g., endemic ethnonationalism, or neofascism—that would make the world look more like it did in past decades, interconnection is likely to deepen and become a defining characteristic of the 21st century. The information revolution is what makes this possible—it provides the capability and the opportunity to circuitize the globe in ways that have never been seen before.

This is likely to be a messy, complicated process, rife with ambivalent, contradictory, and paradoxical effects. It may lead to new patterns of cooperation, competition, *and* conflict across all levels of society (local, national, international), across all spheres of activity (public, private), in all directions (East-West, North-South), all at the same time. It may weaken states in some respects, while strengthening them in others. Ultimately, global interconnection should benefit its proponents, in both state and nonstate arenas; but it may well expose them, and others, to unexpected risks and vulnerabilities along the way. An ambitious actor may have to enter into, and manage, many cross-cutting connections and partnerships—and many of these may involve transnational civil-society actors.

Growing Strength of Global Civil Society. No doubt, states will remain paramount actors in the international system. The information revolution will lead to changes in the nature of the state, but not to its "withering away." What will happen is a transformation.[9] At the

---

[9]There is an ongoing debate about the implications of the information revolution for the future of the state. Our own view is summarized rather than elaborated here.

same time, nonstate actors will continue to grow in strength and influence. This has been the trend for several decades with business corporations and international regulatory regimes. The next trend to expect is a gradual worldwide strengthening of transnational NGOs that represent civil society. As this occurs, there will be a rebalancing of relations among state, market, and civil-society actors around the world—in ways that favor noopolitik over realpolitik.[10]

Realpolitik supposes that states thoroughly define and dominate the international system. This will be less the case as nonstate actors further multiply and gain influence. The top-down strengthening of international regimes, as favored by internationalism, will be only part of the new story. Equally if not more important, from the standpoint of noopolitik, will be the bottom-up strengthening of NGOs that represent civil society.

Noopolitik upholds the importance of nonstate actors, especially from civil society, and requires that they play strong roles. Why? NGOs (not to mention individuals) often serve as sources of ethical impulses (which is rarely the case with market actors), as agents for disseminating ideas rapidly, and as nodes in a networked apparatus of "sensory organizations" that can assist with conflict anticipation, prevention, and resolution. Indeed, largely because of the information revolution, advanced societies are on the threshold of developing a vast sensory apparatus for watching what is happening around the world. This apparatus is not new, because it consists partly of established government intelligence agencies, corporate market-research departments, news media, and opinion-polling firms. What is new is the looming scope and scale of this sensory apparatus, as it increasingly includes networks of NGOs and individual activists who monitor and report on what they see in all sorts of issue areas, using open forums, specialized Internet mailing lists, Web postings, and

---

Some reasons for our view, and literature citations, are provided in Arquilla and Ronfeldt (1996b; and 1997, Ch. 19) and Ronfeldt (1996). Also see Sassen (1998, Ch. 10) and Skolnikoff (1993).

[10]For elaboration of these points, and citations to the literature, see Arquilla and Ronfeldt (1996b) and Ronfeldt (1996). For an early elucidation of the concept of "global civil society," see Frederick (1993a and b). For recent statements, see Slaughter (1997), Simmons (1998), Sassen (1998, Ch. 9), and Clark, Friedman, and Hochstetler (1998).

fax machine ladders as tools for rapid dissemination.[11] For example, early warning is an increasing concern of disaster-relief and humanitarian organizations.

Against this background, the states that emerge strongest in information-age terms—even if by traditional measures they may appear to be smaller, less powerful states—are likely to be the states that learn to work conjointly with the new generation of nonstate actors. Strength may thus emanate less from the "state" per se than from the "system" as a whole. All this may mean placing a premium on state-society coordination, including the toleration of "citizen diplomacy" and the creation of "deep coalitions" between state and civil-society actors (latter term from Toffler and Toffler, 1997). In that sense, it might be said that the information revolution is impelling a shift from a state-centric to a network-centric world (which would parallel a potential shift in the military world from traditional "platform-centric" to emerging "network-centric" approaches to warfare).[12]

This is quite acceptable to noopolitik. While realpolitik remains steadfastly imbued with notions of control, noopolitik is less about control than "decontrol"—perhaps deliberate, regulated decontrol—so that state actors can better adapt to the emergence of independent nonstate actors and learn to work with them through new mechanisms for communication and coordination. Realpolitik would lean toward an essentially mercantilist approach to information as it once did toward commerce; noopolitik is not mercantilist by nature.

Rise of Soft Power. The information revolution, as noted earlier, is altering the nature of power, in large part by making soft power more potent. In the words of Nye, writing with Admiral William Owens (1996, p. 21, referring to Nye, 1990),

---

[11]Schudson (1998, pp. 310–311) argues that it is time for America to give rise to a new (in his historical view, a fourth) model of citizenship that will emphasize civic monitoring. This means environmental surveillance—keeping an eye out—more than it means trying to be knowledgeable about all things (his third model).

[12]The phrase "network-centric" is from military discussions about whether future military operations should be "platform-centric" or "network-centric." See Cebrowski and Garstka (1998).

"Soft power" is the ability to achieve desired outcomes in international affairs through attraction rather than coercion. It works by convincing others to follow, or getting them to agree to, norms and institutions that produce the desired behavior. Soft power can rest on the appeal of one's ideas or the ability to set the agenda in ways that shape the preferences of others.

This does not mean that hard power and realpolitik are obsolete, or even in abeyance. According to Josef Joffe (1997, p. 24),

Let's make no mistake about it. Hard power—men and missiles, guns and ships—still counts. It is the ultimate, because existential, currency of power. But on the day-to-day level, "soft power" . . . is the more interesting coin. . . . Today there is a much bigger payoff in getting others to want what you want, and that has to do with the attraction of one's ideas, with agenda-setting, with ideology and institutions, and with holding out big prizes for cooperation, such as the vastness and sophistication of one's market.

Playing upon a distinction about three different kinds of information—free, commercial, and strategic—Keohane and Nye (1998, p. 94) propose that soft power rests ultimately on credibility, and that this derives mainly from the production and dissemination of free (public) information:

The ability to disseminate free information increases the potential for persuasion in world politics. . . . If one actor can persuade others to adopt similar values and policies, whether it possesses hard power and strategic information may become less important. Soft power and free information can, if sufficiently persuasive, change perceptions of self-interest and thereby alter how hard power and strategic information are used. If governments or NGOs are to take advantage of the information revolution, they will have to establish reputations for credibility amid the white noise of the information revolution.

In our view, the rise of soft power makes noopolitik feasible. Whereas realpolitik often aims at coercion through the exercise of hard power (whose essence is military), noopolitik aims to attract, persuade, coopt, and enjoin with soft power (whose essence is nonmilitary). In keeping with the point that the root *noos* refers to the mind, noopolitik means having a systematic ability to conduct foreign interactions in knowledge-related terms. It requires information strategy to work—indeed, at its indivisible core, noopolitik *is* information strategy.

The relationship between information strategy and the traditional political, military, and economic dimensions of grand strategy can evolve in basically two directions. One is for information strategy to develop as an adjunct or component under each of the traditional dimensions. This process is already under way—as seen, for example, in metaphors about information being a military "force multiplier" and a commercial "commodity" that benefits the United States. The second path—still far from charted—is to develop information strategy as a distinct, new dimension of grand strategy for projecting American power and presence. To accomplish this, information strategists would be well advised to go beyond notions of soft power and consider Susan Strange's (1988, p. 118) related notion of "knowledge structures" as a foundation of power:

> More than other structures, the power derived from the knowledge structure comes less from coercive power and more from consent, authority being conferred voluntarily on the basis of shared belief systems and the acknowledgment of the importance to the individual and to society of the particular form taken by the knowledge— and therefore of the importance of the person having the knowledge and access or control over the means by which it is stored and communicated.

The proponents of realpolitik would probably prefer to stick with treating information as an adjunct of the standard political, military, and economic elements of grand strategy; the very idea of intangible information as a basis for a distinct dimension of strategy seems antithetical to realpolitik. It allows for information strategy as a tool of deception and manipulation (e.g., as in the U.S. deliberate exaggeration of the prospects for its Strategic Defense Initiative during the 1980s). But realpolitik seems averse to accepting "knowledge projection" as amounting to much of a tool of statecraft. However, for noopolitik to take hold, information will have to become a distinct dimension of grand strategy.

We will elaborate later that there is much more to be done in regard to both paths. Our point for now is that the rise of soft power is essential for the emergence of the second path, and thus of noopolitik.

Importance of Cooperative Advantages. States and other actors seek to develop "comparative" advantages. This has mostly meant "competitive" advantages, especially when it comes to great-power rivalries conducted in terms of realpolitik. But, in the information age, "cooperative" advantages will become increasingly important. Moreover, societies that improve their abilities to cooperate with friends and allies may also gain competitive advantages against rivals.

The information revolution and the attendant rise of network forms of organization should improve U.S. competitiveness. But they should also stimulate shifts in the nature of comparative advantage: from its competitive to its cooperative dimensions. An actor's ability to communicate, consult, and coordinate in-depth with other actors may become as crucial as the ability to compete (or engage in conflict) with still other actors. A new interweaving of competitive and cooperative advantages may be expected. This trend is already pronounced in efforts to build regional and global partnerships.

Some U.S. strategists have begun to see the value of "cooperative competition" in regard to global economic, political, and military relations:

> From this network perspective, national strategy will depend less on confrontation with opponents and more on the art of cooperation with competitors. . . . The new strategy of cooperative competition would be defined more in terms of networks of information flows among equals that provide for enhanced cooperation on technological developments and potential responses to international crises in a framework of shifting ad hoc coalitions and intense economic competition. . . . The strategy of the United States, then, would be to play the role of strategic broker, forming, sustaining, and adjusting international networks to meet a sophisticated array of challenges (Golden, 1993, pp. 103, 107, 108).

Thinking along these lines could advance via soft power and noopolitik. In the military area, for example, where advanced information systems give the United States an edge for building international coalitions, "selectively sharing these abilities is therefore not only the route of coalition leadership but the key to maintaining U.S. military superiority" (Nye and Owens, 1996, p. 28). Martin Libicki's (1998 and forthcoming) idea for creating an "open grid" for militarily illuminating the world—a global command, control, communications, computing, intelligence, surveillance, and reconnaissance (C4ISR) system, installed and sustained by the U.S. military, whose information would be available to any country's military so long as it accepts illumination of its own military deployments and other activities—is very much in line with noopolitik. Similar notions are being fielded about global cooperation to address economic, social, judicial, and other issues (e.g., Joffe, 1997; Mathews, 1997; and Slaughter, 1997). David Gompert (1998) argues, more broadly, that freedom and openness are necessary for benefiting fully from the information revolution—and thus a "core" of democratic, market-oriented powers, led by the United States, is gaining a global presence, such that any potentially adversarial power like China who wants to benefit as well from the information revolution will have to adapt to cooperating with this core, including by sharing its interests and eventually its values.[13]

The United States, with its diversity of official, corporate, and civil-society actors, is more disposed and better positioned than other nations to build broad-based, networked patterns of cooperation across all realms of society, and across all societies. This surely means moving beyond realpolitik, which, unlike noopolitik, would avoid information sharing, define issues and options in national rather than global terms, prefer containment to engagement, and focus on threats and defenses rather than on mutual assurances.

Formation of a Global Noosphere. This was discussed at length in the prior chapter. But the point should be reiterated that the formation of a noosphere is crucial for noopolitik. Without the emergence—and deliberate construction—of a massive, well-recognized noosphere, there will be little hope of sustaining the notion that the world is moving to a new system in which "power" is understood mainly in terms of knowledge, and that information strategy should

---

[13]An opinion piece by Ikenberry (1998) articulates a similar set of points, although without tying them to the information revolution.

focus on the "balance of knowledge," as distinct from the "balance of power."

Mutual Relationship Between Realpolitik and Noopolitik

Realpolitik, no matter how modified, cannot be transformed into noopolitik. The two stand in contradiction. This is largely because of the uncompromisingly state-centric nature of realpolitik. It is also because, for an actor to shift the emphasis of its statecraft from realpolitik to noopolitik, there must be a shift from power politics to power-sharing politics. Nonetheless, the contradiction is not absolute; it can, in theory and practice, be made a compatible contradiction (rather like yin and yang). Indeed, true realpolitik depends on the players sharing and responding to some core behavioral values— a bit of noopolitik may thus lie at the heart of realpolitik (see Morgenthau, 1948, pp. 224–231). Likewise, true noopolitik may work best if it accords with power politics—however, this perspective should be less about might makes right, than about right makes might (as also exposited in Gompert, 1998). Understanding this may help in persevering through the transitional period in which realpolitik and noopolitik are likely to coexist. Skillful policymakers and strategists may face choices as to when it is better to emphasize realpolitik or noopolitik, or as to how best to alternate between them or apply hybrids, especially when dealing with a recalcitrant adversary who has been able to resist realpolitik types of pressures.

The relationship between realpolitik and noopolitik may be dynamic in another sense. Patterns of development remain uneven around the world; parts of it are already quite steeped in the dynamics of the information age, while other parts still seem more medieval than modern. Thus, noopolitik will be more pertinent in some parts of the world than in others, and in regard to some issues more than others. We surmise that it will be most pertinent where advanced societies predominate: e.g., in Western Europe and North America. It will be less so where conditions remain traditionally state-centric, and thus ripe for the continuation of realpolitik (e.g., much of Asia). Moreover, noopolitik will be most effective where all manner of media are prevalent, where civil-society NGOs have an edge in generating attention to issues, where government-NGO relations are quite good, and where issues are intricate rather than strictly economic, political, or military.

One way to balance the realpolitik model with aspects of the global interdependence model is to theorize that world politics is bifurcating into two worlds that coexist, overlap, and interact. In this view, as explicated by James Rosenau (1988, 1990), a "multicentric world" of "sovereignty-free" actors concerned with "autonomy" is growing in parallel to the old "state-centric world" of "sovereignty-bound" actors concerned about "security." The latter world corresponds to the traditional nation-state system, the former to the nonstate actors whose numbers, diversity, and influence are increasing—including global corporations, international regimes, and civil-society advocacy groups. This bifurcation may endure a long time and be fraught with major episodes of citizen-based activism, as in the fall of the communist regimes in Eastern Europe,

> where the activists in the population become agents of communication, either through uncoordinated but cumulative behavior or through ad hoc, informal organizational networks (Rosenau, 1992, p. 268).

But even if "bifurcation" makes theoretical sense, a somewhat obverse point is important for the practice of noopolitik: This kind of analysis underscores, again, that noopolitik will require governments to learn to work with civil-society NGOs that are engaged in building cross-border networks and coalitions. Even a geopolitical strategist as traditional as Zbigniew Brzezinski realizes this. At the end of his latest book (1997, p. 215), after treating the world as a "chessboard" to be mastered through statist realpolitik, he turns to postulate that efforts to build a new transnational structure for assuring peace would have the

> advantage of benefiting from the new web of global linkages that is growing exponentially outside the more traditional nation-state system. That web—woven by multinational corporations, NGOs (non-governmental organizations, with many of them transnational in character) and scientific communities and reinforced by the Internet—already creates an informal global system that is inherently congenial to more institutionalized and inclusive global cooperation.

In his view, the United States should work for the creation of such linkages because we are the only ones who can pull this off. Even if U.S. primacy were ultimately to wither away—which is likely in his view—this web of linkages would remain "a fitting legacy of America's role as the first, only, and last truly global superpower."

For cases in which it is not easy to bring realpolitik and noopolitik in line on ethical grounds, and in which there are contradictions and trade-offs that may result in accusations of hypocrisy, the relationship between the two will break down. U.S. policy toward Iraq offers an example. In the 1980s, when Iraq seemed to be losing the Iran-Iraq war, the U.S. government supplied intelligence to Iraq, ignoring Iraq's use of chemical weapons (e.g., in Iraq's 1988 counterattack against Iran on the Faw Peninsula). This was a realpolitik posture. Realpolitik allows for taking the position that a leader may be a heathen but he is "our" heathen—a position that would generally be inconsistent with noopolitik. Today, U.S. policy opposes Iraq's development of chemical weapons on grounds that mix aspects of realpolitik and noopolitik. In other parts of the world—e.g., Algeria, Nigeria, and Saudi Arabia—there also appear to be trade-offs between supporting democracy (an important goal for noopolitik) and supporting an authoritarian or theocratic regime because it rules a country of strategic value (an important goal for realpolitik).

FOSTERING NOOPOLITIK: SOME GUIDELINES AND TASKS

Noopolitik is foreign policy behavior and strategy for the information age that emphasizes the shaping and sharing of ideas, values, norms, laws, and ethics through soft power. Noopolitik is guided more by a conviction that right makes for might, than the obverse. Both state and nonstate actors may be guided by noopolitik; but rather than being state-centric, its strength may likely stem from enabling state and nonstate actors to work conjointly. The driving motivation of noopolitik cannot be national interests defined in statist terms. National interests will still play a role, but they may be defined more in societywide than state-centric terms and be fused with broader, even global, interests in enhancing the transnationally networked "fabric" in which the players are embedded. While realpolitik tends to empower states, noopolitik will likely empower networks of state and nonstate actors. Realpolitik pits one state against another, but noopolitik encourages states to cooperate in coalitions and other mutual frameworks. In all these respects, noopolitik contrasts with realpolitik. Table 2 summarizes this contrast.

Kissinger may be said to epitomize the *zeitgeist* and practice of realpolitik. Who may stand for the zeitgeist of noopolitik? One name that comes to mind is George Kennan. He has always been mindful of realpolitik. Yet, his original notion of containment was not (as he has pointed out many times) essentially military. Rather, it was centered on the idea of creating a community of interests, based on shared ideals, that would secure the free world, while dissuading the Soviet Union from aggression, and eventually persuading it to change. This seems an early expression of noopolitik, geared to a state-centric system. Nelson Mandela and George Soros, not to mention a host of less renowned individuals who have played leading roles in civil-society activist movements, are those whose beliefs and activities reflect the rising importance of nonstate actors.

Some of the best exemplars of the emergence of noopolitik involve "social netwars" waged by civil-society activists (see Arquilla and

Table 2

Contrast Between Realpolitik and Noopolitik

Realpolitik	Noopolitik
States as the unit of analysis	Nodes, nonstate actors
Primacy of hard power (resources, etc.)	Primacy of soft power
Power politics as zero-sum game	Win-win, lose-lose possible
System is anarchic, highly conflictual	Harmony of interests, cooperation
Alliance conditional (oriented to threat)	Ally webs vital to security
Primacy of national self-interest	Primacy of shared interests
Politics as unending quest for advantage	Explicitly seeking a *telos*
Ethos is amoral, if not immoral	Ethics crucially important
Behavior driven by threat and power	Common goals drive actors
Very guarded about information flows	Propensity for info-sharing
Balance of power as the "steady-state"	Balance of responsibilities
Power embedded in nation-states	Power in "global fabric"

Ronfeldt, 1996a and 1997).[14]   While all-out military wars, such as World Wars I and II, represent the conflictual heights (and failures?) of realpolitik, nonmilitary netwars may prove the archetypal conflicts of noopolitik.   The Nobel prize-winning campaign to ban land mines;[15] NGO-led opposition to the Multilateral Agreement on Investment (MAI);[16] the Greenpeace-led campaign against French nuclear testing in the South Pacific; the swarming of transnational NGOs in defense of the Zapatista insurgents in Mexico;[17] and recent information-age efforts by Burmese and Chinese dissidents, with support from U.S.-based NGOs, to press for human rights and political reforms in these countries[18] all exemplify how transnational civil-society networks, in some cases with strong support from states, can practice noopolitik, with varying degrees of success, to change the policies of states that persist in emphasizing the traditional politics of power.   These cases substantiate that old ideas about "peace through strength" may give way to new ideas of "peace through knowledge."   They also show that ideas themselves, particularly ones with deep ethical appeal, may be fused with advanced communications technologies and new organizational designs to create a new model of power and diplomacy that governments will increasingly encounter and have to heed.   Noopolitik is more attuned than realpolitik to the advent of social netwar.   And for now, activist NGOs, perhaps because they lack the resources for realpolitik, appear to be

---

[14]Netwar is an information-age entry on the spectrum of conflict that is defined by the use of network forms of organization, doctrine, and strategy, made possible by the information revolution. We presume here that most readers are familiar with the concept. See Arquilla and Ronfeldt (1996a, 1997).

[15]For an academic analysis of this movement that treats moral suasion and organizational networking as important factors in the growth of transnational civil society, see Price (1998).

[16]Kobrin (1998) views this opposition to the MAI as a "clash of globalizations"—between the type of globalization favored by investors, and a newer type represented by electronically networked global civil society actors who oppose economic globalization.

[17]On the Zapatista movement in Mexico, see Cleaver (1998) and Ronfeldt et al. (1998).

[18]On Burma, see Danitz and Strobel (forthcoming).   On China, see dissidents' declarations posted at sites maintained by Human Rights in China (www.hrichina.org) and the Digital Freedom Network (www.dfn.org). Periodic articles in The *Los Angeles Times* have also provided excellent coverage of efforts by Chinese dissidents to use the Internet to spread their views.

ahead of states in having the motivation and ability to apply noopolitik.

But what if states regard noopolitik as attractive, without caring about the emergence and construction of the noosphere? In the hands of a democratic leader, noopolitik might then amount to little more than airy, idealistic rhetoric with little or no structural basis; while, in the hands of a dictator or a demagogue, it could be reduced to manipulative propaganda.[19]   Or narrow versions of noopolitik may be practiced mainly for private gain—in the commercial worlds of advertising and public relations, this already occurs when companies develop a media blitz and plant testimonials to shape public opinion.

Much as the rise of realpolitik depended on the development and exploitation of the geosphere (whose natural resources enhance state power), so will the rise of noopolitik depend on the development and exploitation of the noosphere. To pursue this, measures need to be identified that, in addition to fostering the rise of a noosphere, are likewise geared to facilitating the effectiveness of soft power, the deepening of global interconnections, the strengthening of transnational civil-society actors, and the creation of conditions for governments to be better able to act conjointly (in terms of cooperative advantages), especially with nonstate actors.

The following are some measures for U.S. policy and strategy that could assist with the development of the noosphere and noopolitik. All are taken from ongoing discussions about issues raised by the advance of the information revolution.

- Continue to support expansion of cyberspace connection around the world. Support the access of NGOs as well as state and mar-

---

[19]It has been suggested that a Hitler would like the concept of noopolitik. Our rejoinder is that noopolitik must be based on the existence of a noosphere, and that the openness and interconnectedness that comes with a noosphere would expose and constrain a Hitler. Additionally, some religious and other cults may practice a version of noopolitik to attract adherents and assail their critics and opponents, although at base these cultists operate from a closed, even isolating ethos that really contradicts the notion of an open, global noosphere.

ket actors to it, including where this runs counter to the preferences of authoritarian regimes.[20]

- Move away from realpolitik designs to control encryption, toward freedom of encryption. (For a good discussion, see Dyson, 1997.)

- To ensure cyberspace safety and security at the international level, develop multitiered information systems for information sharing, creating a shared infosphere.[21]

- Promote freedom of information and communications as a right. Article 19 of the Universal Declaration of Human Rights states that "everyone has a right to seek, receive and impart information and ideas through any media and regardless of frontiers." An equivalent appears in the International Covenant for Civil and Political Rights. Noopolitik requires more. Activists on the political left have drafted a "Peoples Communications Charter."[22] Something along these lines, made suitable for people across the political spectrum, seems essential for the evolution of a global noosphere.[23]

- Encourage the creation of "special media forces." They might be modeled along the lines of special forces units but should be armed with weapons of the media (e.g., digital cameras and satellite uplinks) rather than those of the military. Under some circumstances, they could be dispatched into conflict zones to

---

[20]See Kedzie (1997) for the argument that communication, interconnection, and democracy reinforce each other.

[21]This point is from a briefing by RAND colleague Robert H. Anderson.

[22]See http://www.waag.org/pcc/. Also see Frederick (1993b).

[23]This point, with variations, has adherents in Japan, as well as in America and Europe. Kumon and Aizu (1993, p. 318) write:

> [T]he emergence of hypernetwork society will require not only physical/technical infrastructure but also a wide range of new social agreements binding the infostructure that is the social/human network. We propose that the core of such infostructure will be "information rights," a new concept of human rights that will supplement, and in part replace, property rights that have been widely accepted in modern industrial society.

Also see Frederick (1993a), in the same book.

help settle disputes through the discovery and dissemination of accurate information.[24]

- Open diplomacy to greater coordination between state and nonstate actors, especially NGOs, by undertaking a "revolution in diplomatic affairs" (RDA) that matches the revolutions under way in business and military affairs (see Arquilla and Ronfeldt, 1997 and 1998b).[25]

- Broach with other potentially interested state and nonstate actors the idea of building an "information commonwealth" (term from Cooper, 1997, and other sources).[26]

These measures relate to the creation of a global noosphere that would be of interest to all realms of society. It may also be advisable for the United States to work on creating a "military noosphere"—and for that, different measures may be needed. The goals might include improving jointness in the U.S. military, as well as the effectiveness of the U.S. military engagement, alliance, and coalition activities abroad, and U.S. ability to address small scale contingencies (SSCs) involving NGOs. The emphasis in recent years on "jointness" among the U.S. armed services could be a key aspect of the creation of a military noosphere. In a similar light, the many foreign internal defense (FID) missions of U.S. forces throughout the world (in over 100 countries) could be seen as external aspects of an emerging military noosphere.

---

[24]For related ideas, also see Metzl (1997), De Caro (1996), and Toffler and Toffler (1993). An earlier idea, fielded by Anderson and Shapiro (1992), is that of creating "deployable local networks to reduce conflict," which could be rushed into conflict situations in the expectation that increased communications may foster conflict resolution. Still earlier, Keohane (1984, p. 121) proposed that "data sovereignty," if it could be established, would ease environmental debates.

[25]For background on the prospects for an RDA, and on the concept of "virtual diplomacy," see materials from the conference on "Virtual Diplomacy: The Global Communications Revolution and International Conflict Management," organized by the U.S. Institute for Peace, Washington, D.C., April 1–2, 1997, located at http://www.usip.org/. Also see Cambone (1996), Shultz (1997), Solomon (1997), Wriston (1997), The Project on the Advocacy of U.S. Interests Abroad (1998), and Burt, Robison, and Fulton (1998).

[26]Benedict Anderson's (1991) notion of an "imagined community" may be appropriate, too.

In a sense, a military noosphere is already emerging, although no one has yet called it that. In addition, no one has thought through the ideational, organizational, strategic, and technological implications of this emergence. An overarching aim of military noopolitik might be to supersede realpolitik's emphasis on "strong defenses" with a new emphasis on "strong sharing," which may avoid accusations that the military noosphere is only a new name for an old approach to domination—realpolitik in disguise. A traditional realpolitik mind-set makes it difficult to share with others and could thus encourage an "information arms race." However, in today's world, a failure to engage in strong sharing with friends and allies, in regard to such issues as cyberspace security and safety, may undermine the prospects for either realpolitik or noopolitik.

If a U.S.-led military noosphere can be built, the key gains may be in peacetime rather than wartime, for such purposes as conflict anticipation and prevention, nation-building, humanitarian and disaster relief, and confidence-building with regard to new military and security arrangements in various parts of the world. Libicki's notion, mentioned earlier, of an "open grid"—a global C4ISR system open to all—could provide a structural element for a military noosphere. Success with designing a military model of the noosphere might lead the way for creation of a diplomatic counterpart.

As U.S. information strategy approaches the rise of the noosphere and noopolitik it should be based on "guarded openness." This is an advisable policy posture for democracies (Arquilla and Ronfeldt, 1996b and 1997). Openness is crucial for sharing, which is the ethical and practical essence of the noosphere and noopolitik, but guardedness will long remain crucial for security. Most of the general measures noted above emphasize openness, but military noosphere measures will require a different balance between openness and guardedness. The next chapter goes more deeply into military and security matters, where achieving the best balance between guardedness and openness—and between the enduring value of realpolitik and the emerging value of noopolitik—may require a deft hand in the years ahead.

As all this gets worked out, it may become clear that there is a lot more to noopolitik than merely asserting, sharing, and instituting the particular values, norms, ethics, laws, and other ingredients of soft power that an actor wants to uphold. What may especially matter for all parties—the advocates and their audiences—is the "story" that is being told, implicitly or explicitly.[27]   Realpolitik is typically about whose military or economy wins. Noopolitik may ultimately be about whose story wins.

---

[27]Thus, further analytical elaboration of noopolitik may benefit from inquiring into the "postmodernist" literature about the importance of narrative and discourse in the exercise of power, as exemplified by the writings of Michel Foucault and Jacques Derrida; and into a new academic literature about story modeling, as exemplified by Pennington and Hastie (1986). We are indebted to RAND colleague Tanya Charlick-Paley for calling the story-modeling literature to our attention.

Chapter Four

INTERNATIONAL COOPERATION AND CONFLICT

This chapter considers selected policy-relevant implications of the emergence of noopolitik that are likely to influence the development of American information strategy. The analysis first examines various ways in which the traditional political, economic, and military domains of grand strategy may be affected, especially in terms of the prospects for broadening and deepening international cooperation. Next, the role of information strategy in crisis and conflict is examined, both in terms of the importance of new forms of public diplomacy and the need to craft an integrated strategic information doctrine (SID) to guide the management of informational capabilities and resources in wartime.

INFORMATION STRATEGY AND GLOBAL COOPERATION

Because the very notion of a noosphere is global, it should be apparent from the outset that success in actualizing this realm of the mind depends upon the ability to enlist others—from states, to NGOs, to "deep coalitions" of the two—to cooperate in support of it. In thinking about how to build cooperation, we have modified classical notions about grand strategy to reflect the sensibilities implied by the rise of noopolitik.

Thus, economic strategy should be fused with legal structures and norms as the global economy grows ever more reliant upon ideas and knowledge products and practices for its growth and health. In the military realm, it will likewise be increasingly important to move beyond traditional quantitative measures of military effectiveness, in which one party's strength threatens another. Instead, military issues are viewed as tied inextricably to mutual security—placing the need for cooperation in this realm at a premium. Indeed, in a noopolitik world—even one that must coexist with substantial realpolitik elements—militaries that are attractive as partners, rather than feared as hegemons, are more likely to craft robust mutual security arrangements.

With regard to the political means and ends of traditional grand strategy, the realist and neorealist days of state-monopolized "high politics" (see Morgenthau, 1948; Waltz, 1979) are likely numbered, as the rise of nonstate actors and the emergence of a global civil society bring the social dimension of world politics to the fore. Thus, the tight coupling between social and political affairs will feature the active participation—sometimes the predominance—of nonstate civil (and uncivil) society actors.

These modified spheres of grand strategy each afford glimpses into how information strategy may complement the traditional tools of statecraft. But they also show how information strategy might emerge as a distinct dimension of statecraft as well. Note that the following discussion is exemplary rather than exhaustive. Our goal at this point is simply to sketch out the types of policy issues likely to rise in each realm, and the manner in which information strategy may help to foster cooperation and deter conflict.

Finally, it is important to recognize that some blurring and/or blending of the realms is likely to occur. For example, while the diffusion of legal norms and practices will be closely interwoven with economic affairs in a noopolitik world, normative institutions and practices will be visible in the other realms as well. While not likely to take on the same degree of statutory penetration as in economics and trade, military-security and sociopolitical affairs will no doubt be more influenced by ethical considerations in a noopolitik world. This does not change the point that the principal effect of new legal paradigms will be felt in the world economy. It just suggests the permeability of the "membrane" that divides our strategic analytic constructs.

The Economic-Legal Realm

In the economic-legal sphere, the primary concerns are commercial. Given the explosive growth of international trade and finance, especially in cyberspace, ensuring the safety and security of flows of goods and transactions necessarily forms the foundation for cooperation. From an economic-legal perspective, this cooperation may depend upon reaching agreement in several issue areas, beginning with what might be called "substantive law." This notion basically calls for agreement as to what constitutes a "crime," including fraud, forgery, hacking, and sabotage (or, as we have called it, "cybotage").

Cooperation may also hinge upon acceptance of a body of administrative and legal procedure that would establish jurisdiction and allow enforcement of the substantive laws designed to protect property and other assets, both in and out of cyberspace. In the information realm, agreement about such matters as territoriality, extradition, and the notion of "hot pursuit" may form a minimum basis for international cooperation. The challenge will be to harmonize these bases for cooperation—especially in the area of cyberspace-based territoriality—with the noosphere.

Information strategy will likely play a key role in transnational law enforcement, since any information-age "policing paradigm" would rely heavily upon regular flows of information among law enforcement bodies. Although police agencies are indeed showing signs that they recognize the importance of networking, it may be that some sort of clearinghouse will be needed to facilitate cooperation. At a policy level, it might even be useful to build on the Interpol model, adding to it an "Infopol" specializing in dealing with cyberspace-based criminal activities, to help optimize the benefits of already existing police information management operations.

The current multilateral law enforcement regime (e.g., Interpol) is built on significant information sharing, and a great deal of coordination, both formally (in state-to-state treaties or agreements) and informally (in terms of day-to-day interactions of policing organizations). A policing paradigm should also provide a grassroots basis for broadening the role of international courts of law in the informational domain—a key principle in building a global noosphere. As desirable as this approach seems, it would have difficulty in dealing with the problem of noncompliance by recalcitrant states asserting their sovereign rights. Thus, this framework would also have to include significant intelligence capabilities to identify and cope with the problem of noncompliance.

The most serious aspect of noncooperation would be that just a few "defectors" from the envisioned international regime, providing "havens" for malefactors, could compromise overall information security, damaging the global economy and weakening nascent international legal cooperation. This difficulty could arise if a state decided that its national interests overrode commitments to some international "public good." Alternately, some nonstate actors (e.g., transnational criminal organizations, or TCOs) might have little reason to cooperate with multilateral agreements. Indeed, these nonstate actors might profit by defying the cooperative regime; and they might then attract some states to align with them, providing "pirate nets" to provide for their information infrastructural requirements.

Also, some states might be motivated to support defiance of an international cooperative regime simply because they fear the growth of transnational, or possibly supranational, authority—or because they feel that the "wiring of the world" might simply make the rich nations richer, widening the gap between the "haves" and "have-nots." Thus, efforts to knit together an information-driven economic-legal regime might engender its own "backlash," which might also affect the military-security realm. Finally, even among states inclined to cooperate, there might be reluctance to agree to a regime in which, say, encryption afforded a great degree of protection to electronic commerce, but only at the price of allowing supranational bodies that would act as "key escrow agents." The other side of this issue is that many states might balk, as the United States has, at the notion of providing unbreakable encryption to individuals and commercial concerns, since this would restrict the surveillance capabilities (and therefore, the power) of the state. If U.S. policymakers are to be persuaded to encourage and nurture the development of the noosphere, the potential constraints that a global noosphere would impose upon American power would have to be carefully analyzed and weighed against the overall benefits.

Concerning advanced hardware, however, there is eagerness, throughout the world, to see the diffusion of high-performance computers (HPCs). The United States has a controlling position in the world market; therefore, the economic gains from wide sales of these machines are substantial. However, HPCs can also be used as a covert means to refine nuclear devices, as well as to aid in the development of other arms, including strategic information warfare weaponry. Thus, the tension in this case between prospects for commercial gain and new worries about weapons diffusion will likely be managed only by an information strategy designed to maintain the equilibrium between competing economic and security values.

Currently, official U.S. policy leans heavily toward openness—in large part because of early assessments that guardedness was infeasible in this area, since the United States is not able to control the diffusion of HPC technology (Goodman, Wolcott, and Burkhart, 1995). This view has been disputed (Arquilla, 1996), and the General Accounting Office, after conducting its own study of the matter, has recently concluded that more-guarded approaches are indeed workable.[1] The key point from this example is that, by adopting a strategy grounded in guarded openness, policymakers might become habituated to seeking out "blended" solutions, and become less susceptible to assessments that rule out from the start either of these aspects of information strategy.

Military-Security Affairs

A major dimension of grand strategy—and of information strategy in particular—is military-security issues. International cooperation in protecting and securing the use of cyberspace and other means of communicating vital information will be necessary for transnational defense. In this realm, it may be necessary to articulate a new vision in which a robust variant of "common defense" will emerge as a top priority to enable both collective security and coalition warfare in the future. Common defense, in terms of information strategy, refers to the notion that all members of a security regime or alliance must have similarly strong remedies against threats to their information infrastructures. Because of the deeply interconnected nature of information security, compromise of one sector could have serious ef-

---

[1]See Jeff Gerth, "U.S. Agency Faults Study on Exports of Computers," *The New York Times*, September 17, 1998.

fects upon the whole—the chain is only as strong as its weakest link. This implies less "slack" than sometimes existed in Cold War–era collective security regimes, which often had wide disparities in capabilities, and in which deterrence and defense rested on the ability of the strongest partner(s) to defend against aggression. In the future, a compromise in information security of even a smaller member of a coalition might cripple efforts to deal with an attacker. Therefore, information security must be seen of paramount importance to military affairs.

Specifically, common defense would need to be able to cope with three types of threats. First, the alliance's information infrastructure would have to feature sufficient robustness to ensure that disruptive actions, in cyberspace and out, could not seriously compromise the deployment or projection of military forces in a timely manner. A second related, and equally nettlesome, concern relates to the need to guard against cyberspace and other attacks that might be used in conjunction with a subversive insurgent or revolutionary movement, either an internal or external one. The risk in this case would be that a key node in a common defense network might be "brought down" by actions that might not ever be identified as those of an external aggressor.

Finally, global cooperation for information security would also have to address the problem of protection against lesser "pinprick" attacks (for example, by cyberterrorists) on members of the alliance or coalition. Such attacks may be aimed at wearing down the will to engage in an intervention, or to continue an ongoing fight, and represent something of an information-age variant of what the early air power theorists, Douhet (1942) and De Seversky (1942), thought could be achieved with the aerial bombardment of civilian targets. The similarity between the air power theory and lesser attacks on cyberspace infrastructure lies in the vulnerability of a civil population to either air (including missile) or cyberspace attacks, despite the fact that its armed forces have not been defeated in the field.

This vision of the complex military-security dimension of information strategy may face problems on two levels. First, establishing a true "common defense" structure would require the sharing of a great deal of sensitive, proprietary information among alliance and coalition members, and perhaps even with informally aligned "friends." In an era when allies may later become enemies (e.g., Syria during the Gulf Crisis, and subsequently), the need to disseminate information coupled with the possibility of having only conditionally loyal or inconstant allies pose a dilemma. And, if this concern impedes the development of a collaborative security regime, then not sharing sensitive data may spark an information "arms race"—a competition to develop tools for offensive information warfare—even among putative allies. Thus, there must be both guardedness, to avoid undue security risks, but also enough openness and sharing of sensitive information and technologies to provide disincentives to others to commence such an arms race. Clearly, information arms races would be inimical to the goal of building a global noosphere.

A second concern that could cloud global cooperation in the military-security realm involves the rise of nonstate actors. It is possible that the nature of combatants will blur in future wars, with many participants having principal allegiances to ethnic, religious, or revolutionary movements rather than to nation-states. The tendrils of these organizations will reach into, among, and between states, making these malefactors hard to deter or defend against. TCOs also fall into this category, with their potential to engage in "strategic crime" against a state's political, economic, and social institutions (e.g., in Colombia and, to a lesser degree, in Russia).

The Sociopolitical Arena

In the sociopolitical sphere, unlike in the previous realms, there may be a much more robust, global harmony of interests. Indeed, it is possible that, with the rise of a global civil society, a cooperative noosphere might arise and be sustained even in the absence of strong intergovernmental participatory regimes. This prospect can be characterized as a new "optimistic hypothesis," updating Lipset's (1960) idea of prosperity fostering the advance of democracy. In this newer formulation, interconnectivity would have a democratizing influence on all societies. Thus, the ideal future may be one in which free speech is protected as a public good and is disseminated widely to ever freer audiences. However, it is important to underscore the point that this is a hypothesis—one that might be undermined or falsified by the rise of antidemocratic influences that take advantage of interconnectivity to sow seeds of repression and distrust rather than of transnational harmony.

Thinking strategically regarding the prospect of democratic social evolution via free flows of information through a burgeoning noosphere, we must note that such flows could create permissive conditions for the waging of activist "social netwars" designed to disrupt state stability and control. On one hand, it is possible to argue that such disruption, aimed at an authoritarian state, is ultimately beneficial. On the other hand, both moral and practical dilemmas would be posed by the near-term disruption of friendly, even if authoritarian, states. Lastly, the ethical guidance provided by a noopolitik perspective on statecraft should impel states to ask whether to allow themselves to be used as sanctuaries for those who attack other states.

Building Global Cooperation

The development of American information strategy, especially in support of building a cooperative global noosphere, requires that the major paths ahead be identified. Two stand out. One path consists of a widespread grassroots effort to foster cooperation from the bottom up. This approach would rely heavily upon contributions from and leadership of NGOs and a variety of other civil society actors; it would also presume upon states to relax their hold on sovereignty. The second path would take a top-down approach, relying upon either the hegemonic stability afforded by a leading power (e.g., the United States is seen by many as providing, by virtue of its matchless power, the basis for a liberal international economic order), or the primacy of such international governmental organizations as the United Nations and the Organization for Economic Cooperation & Development.

Each approach would seek to create an expanding web of cooperation. We note that similar methods—and goals—can be seen in earlier eras. With regard to the rise of market economies, there was the interplay of top-down and bottom-up forces, particularly from the beginning of the age of oceanic discovery in the 16th century. During this era, great trading states sought to expand global trade, often linking with growing regional trading regimes. However, this created a great deal of tension as the great maritime states soon sought to bend the market to their parochial interests—leading to the highly competitive, conflictual era of mercantilism. Eventually, bottom-up market forces helped to overturn mercantilist tendencies (see Schumpeter, 1954; von Mises, 1957; North, 1981; Rosecrance, 1984).

A similar pattern existed in the realm of power politics, beginning with the emergence of the modern international system—which also started at the dawn of the 16th century. During this period, great empires strove to bring order from the top down. At the same time, local actors often contrived bottom-up balances of power that created small, but often growing, spheres of peace and order. The Italian city-states of this period, in fact, served as the inspiration for the modern notion of the balance of power. However, as in the economic case, the great powers became imperialist in outlook, causing sharp conflicts. A centuries-long struggle between top-down efforts to impose order and grassroots independence movements ensued, with the empires slowly losing ground, until the last, the Soviet Union, dissolved in 1991 (Dehio, 1961; Kennedy, 1987).

These examples from the past suggest that information strategy will likely develop along multiple paths. There may be incentives to achieve order through a top-down process: (1) American primacy; (2) central institutions, such as the World Court and the United Nations; or (3) alliances of leading states, such as NATO. There will also be grassroots efforts to build a global noosphere from the bottom up, led principally by nonstate actors, especially NGOs. And, just as the market economics and power politics of the past featured tensions between the two approaches to establishing order and cooperation, there will likely be similar frictions in the information age. For example, encouraging a benevolent American hegemony may spark resistance; the United Nations may be hamstrung by the loss of consensus among those with veto power; and NATO's expanding web of security may encourage unruly counterbalancing responses. Indeed, the many constraints on top-down approaches leave room for noosphere-building by nonstate—particularly global civil society—actors.

However, some states, confronted with this challenge to their control of the international system, may act in concert to try to delimit the influence of NGOs. Whether such states succeed in suppressing the rise of the noosphere—or have sufficient motivation even to try—

seems problematic. A far more productive approach would be for states to recognize the comparative advantages of working with, rather than against, NGOs. In this insight lie the beginnings of a true revolution in diplomatic affairs.

To cope with these sorts of problems, a skillful blending of the top-down and bottom-up methods may help in sidestepping the pitfalls of conflict and threat. Such a hybrid strategy would likely feature use of American political, economic, and military capabilities to deliberately empower nonstate actors—including by bringing them into the United Nations (Toffler and Toffler, 1997). In some ways, this strategy is analogous to the Cold War–era strengthening of war-torn Western Europe and Japan against the communist threat—as the United States used its power to build up others, even to the point of creating new economic giants that could rival its own market power.

There are risks in such a strategy. A vibrant, NGO-led global civil society might one day effectively curtail the exercise of American power in some arenas. Yet, if free flows of information do indeed foster democracy and open markets, the benefits of such a strategy are likely to exceed the liabilities. However, even as the United States leads in the creation of what some in (and out of) government are calling an "information commonwealth" (e.g., Cooper, 1997), it must also be remembered that the emerging norms of noopolitik will rise and take hold in a world rife with the conflicts endemic to realpolitik.

INFORMATION STRATEGY IN CRISIS AND CONFLICT

In addition to addressing the uses of information strategy in peacetime, it is also necessary to examine the strategic utility of information in crisis and conflict. With this in mind, this section focuses on two major dimensions of information strategy: public diplomacy and strategic information warfare. The former consists primarily of the use of the "content" aspect of information to influence behavior of an adversary—whether a mass public, a specific leader, or both (on this, see Manheim, 1994). The latter comprises the efforts to strike at an enemy's information conduits (from military command and control to industrial and other infrastructures) by principally electronic means (Molander, Riddile, and Wilson, 1996). Also, we note that although public diplomacy is most useful in crisis, it may also prove effective in wartime. In addition, strategic information warfare strikes, although clearly intended for use in wartime, might also have great preemptive effect if used during a crisis. For those reasons, it is time now to develop a strategic information doctrine to help guide and govern the use of public diplomacy and information warfare in crisis and conflict.

The Role of Public Diplomacy

In the area of public diplomacy, we consider several key issues. First, to have truly strategic (i.e., lasting) effect, initiatives in this area should be based on the truth. This is already a fundamental tenet of the American practice of psychological operations, as can be seen in Joint Publication 3-53, *Doctrine for Psychological Operations.* But it must be noted that others have, in the past, found great value in the use of falsehoods—seeking strategic leverage through deception. During the Cold War, the Soviet Union adopted this approach for psychological operations, which were often effective for long periods of time (see Radvanyi, 1990). In our view, an approach based on falsehoods will more likely have only short-term, or tactical effects— not enduring strategic ones. Therefore, truth must be the polestar of American strategic public diplomacy, and uses of information as "propaganda" should be eschewed.

The effective use of public diplomacy will likely hinge upon the ability of nation-states to reach out to and form "deep coalitions" (term from Toffler and Toffler, 1997) with NGOs. In this way U.S. public diplomacy would be complemented by the actions of countless supporters operating on behalf of an emerging global civil society steeped in American-oriented values: democracy, human rights, and social, political, and economic liberalism. A key doctrinal question is, What should be done when global civil society differs in its aims from what are thought to be key American interests? The answer to this question is two-part.

First, U.S. information strategy could determine whether civil society actors are divided or largely united in their views. If divided, then the clear strategy is to reach out to those most congenial to the American position and to ally with them to help shape the world perceptual environment. Second, if there were widespread opposition to an American policy position, there may be a need to reconsider the policy itself. The goal would be to amend it so as to bring policy more into line with the preferences of civil society. Failure to do so would greatly hamper the ability to continue using public diplomacy in the given issue area.

An example of this sort of problem is the U.S. policy in response to the global civil society effort to ban land mines. U.S. leaders, keenly aware of the broad international consensus on the ban, and the unanimity among the NGOs, strove to soften the American position by seeking a phaseout over a 10-year period, with an exception made for the Korean peninsula. These marginal adjustments to U.S. policy had little effect on the activities of the movement to ban land mines—which have led to the signing of a multilateral treaty by over 100 countries. The United States has refused to sign it, mainly for military reasons. Yet, if the United States were to reconsider its position on this issue it could focus on rethinking the military's reliance on land mines, either in the form of shifting to new maneuver doctrines that have little utility for land mines or in the form of developing mobile mines that will move along with ground troops. Either solution would resolve the issue, and both may lead to better military doctrines.

The key point is that when faced with serious and sustained opposition from global civil society (and by many nation-states also) to a particular policy, America will not find that public diplomacy alone will prevail in the arena of international discourse. It will be necessary, in cases like these, to reconsider the policy in question very carefully and to let the world know that reassessment is under way.

Strategic Information Doctrine (SID)

From the 1997 report of the President's Commission on Critical Infrastructure Protection and the emerging spate of government, military, and academic studies, it seems clear that most analysts accept the argument that strategic information warfare (SIW)—electronic attack against communications, transport, and other key nodes—has emerged as a threat to U.S. national security. While there is some concern about threats from other nations, the basic American view is that this type of war, or cyberterror, will be commonly wielded by nonstate adversaries. Abroad, we also see that there is international consensus about this threat to foreign assets as well—however, foreign (especially Russian and Chinese) views of SIW generally see the United States as the serious threat (Thomas, 1997; Arquilla and Karmel, 1997).

Against this backdrop, incentives are growing for the United States to move toward the development of a "wartime" strategic information doctrine (SID) to complement its peacetime approaches to perception management and public diplomacy.   To date, strategic thinking in this issue area is redolent with nuclear-era concepts. With regard to defense, it has been argued by the President's Commission on Critical Infrastructure Protection and others (e.g., see Molander, Riddile, and Wilson, 1996) that a "minimum essential information infrastructure" (MEII) be created. This notion has clear roots in the nuclear-era minimum essential emergency communication network (MEECN). On the offensive side, SIW is seen as consisting of strikes that aim at countervalue or counterforce targets—either in massive or proportionate retaliatory fashion.

The nuclear analogy will likely prove to be an insufficient basis for developing a clear strategic framework for waging information warfare. The differences between nuclear war and SIW are too great, beginning with the overwhelming destructive power of nuclear weapons, whose very lethality has made deterrence strong for over 50 years. By comparison, SIW is basically disruptive rather than destructive. Furthermore, the nuclear "club" remains small and is still composed of states only, while SIW does not require the wherewithal of a state.   Moreover, it is extremely unlikely that a nuclear attack could be undertaken anonymously, or deniably. SIW is characterized by the inherent ease with which perpetrators may maintain their anonymity.

A final difference between the two is that even today, over half a century into the nuclear age, defenses remain minimal and problematic (partly a result of political decisions not to develop robust defenses during the Cold War).[2] In the area of information security, however, good—although certainly not leakproof—defenses have been identifiable from the outset. As to the current state of defenses of the information infrastructure, Willis Ware has put it succinctly, "There is no evidence that 'the sky is falling'" (1998, p. vii).

---

[2]This point is highlighted by the recent (May 1998) failures in field experiments held to test the efficacy of a theater high-altitude area defense (THAAD).

In the case of SIW, the effort to look ahead, doctrinally, is not likely to be well rewarded by looking back to the nuclear paradigm—save perhaps for the exception provided by the nuclear "no first use" concept, as discussed below. Instead, there must be fresh theorizing about the nature and scope of SIW, which must then be related to American national security needs. What are these needs? On the defensive, or guarded side, the United States must develop a robust information security regime that protects both the ability to project military force abroad and the key nodes that sustain the American way of life at home.

The MEII, as originally conceptualized, is not likely to achieve a secure infosphere for either of these needs. The MEII allows much of the United States to remain wide open to disruption; it also misses the point that present military reliance upon civilian communications means that an insecure civilian sector imperils American military capabilities. However, broad use of strong encryption will substantially improve the defenses of both the civilian and military sectors from the threat posed by SIW.[3] An important recent development has been the effort to rethink the very notions of what constitutes a "minimum" information infrastructure, and what indeed is "essential." This line of discussion holds out the promise that it will be possible to create layers of information security that vary across those areas where there is either a substantial or a poor ability to control access and use (Anderson et al., forthcoming).

On the more proactive side, the United States should develop a SID that eschews first use of information attacks on others. In this regard, SIW features many of the moral dilemmas that were part of the emergence of strategic air power (e.g., see Arquilla, forthcoming).

Generally speaking, an ethical imperative to avoid first use of SIW could actually have practical benefits. This is the case because the United States has the largest set of information targets in the world— and will continue to do so for the foreseeable future. In this regard,

---

[3]It must be recognized that the price of diffusing strong encryption throughout cyberspace will decrease government ability to gain access to private communications. FBI director Louis Freeh has been the most articulate opponent of widespread diffusion of strong encryption tools, citing the limiting effect it would have on criminal investigations. However, examination of all federal prosecutions in 1996 indicates that less than one one-hundredth of a percent of these cases employed cybertaps.

an American information strategy aimed at mounting normative prohibitions on the use of SIW could form a powerful step in the direction of fostering noopolitik. But, as desirable as this might be, a convention on no first use (one of the few nuclear-age concepts that does have information-age relevance) would also hinder the United States from using SIW as a preemptive tool in a crisis or conflict situation.

The solution to this moral dilemma may lie in the medieval Thomist "just-war" formulation about the need to balance the benefits of an act against the harm done. Seen in this light, the United States might then introduce doctrinal nuances, such as reserving the right to use information attack first only if the adversary has already begun to use other forms of force—and if the initiator of SIW has the clear intent to engage in information operations as a means to foreshorten military operations.

In sum, a strategic information doctrine for crisis and conflict should be built around two doctrines. First, to defend and protect against information attacks, emphasis should be placed on a regime where the most advanced encryption is disseminated widely. Second, regarding offensive SIW, doctrine must be driven by the constraints of an ethical noopolitik—with the benefit that placing constraints on first use will likely have practical positive effects. These are key strategic issues for information doctrine in crisis and war that can and should form the core of thinking about defense against, as well as use of, SIW.

Chapter Five

MOVING AHEAD

This report has argued for the development of an American information strategy based on noopolitik. The information revolution has already deepened and diffused to such a degree that other actors—both state and nonstate—have begun to incorporate informational elements into their own strategies. The spread of the information revolution beyond the United States foreshadows an era in which many actors will be competing over who has an "information edge" (Nye and Owens, 1996), as well as over who is "bound to lead" the international system (Nye, 1990). There is no assurance that the United States will necessarily assume or sustain such a role. Despite all of America's advances in the technological realm, only strategies applied wisely will enable their potential to be realized. Thus, whether the United States wants to or not, it must think strategically about the role of information in statecraft.

A NEW TURN OF MIND

The key to making information strategy a workable, distinct tool of statecraft lies in learning to benefit from the emergence of a global noosphere. Without an unbounded, global "realm of the mind," it will be difficult to project "information power" to the distant locales and into the many situations where it is likely to prove useful. Just what building a global noosphere means is not yet clear. But, in our view, it consists less of expanding cyberspace and the infosphere, and much more of building new institutional and organizational links. These might take the form of increasing juridical recognition of NGOs (perhaps even to the point of giving them seats in the

United Nations, as the Tofflers have suggested). It also likely means that traditional approaches to diplomacy may have to be upended, to be replaced by a revolution in diplomatic affairs.[1]

The best possibilities for U.S. information strategy gravitate toward fostering openness. But what of guardedness? While we noted in Chapter Four some of the areas in which guardedness is a preferred policy (e.g., protection of intellectual property and sharing sensitive data with semi-trusted allies), it is important to realize that guardedness can coexist with openness. Thus, the United States may be quite open with semi-trusted allies, even though there will be some types of very sensitive information that ought not to be shared with them. Finally, while something will often be held back, in information strategy the overall balance between being open and being guarded is more likely to be weighted in favor of openness.

In addition, a symbiotic relationship exists between information strategy and the other tools of statecraft. It seems clear that information strategy can improve military performance, increase economic efficiency (whether via markets or sanctions), and aid diplomatic processes. What are less clear are the effects that political, economic, and military initiatives might have on information strategy. For example, a particular policy aimed at encouraging the liberalization of an authoritarian society, by means of increasing its interconnectivity, might actually be undermined if that same society were suffering under economic sanctions designed to close it off from the rest of the world. The same sort of reservations might be applicable to the case of using military demonstrations or shows of force to try to coerce a desired response. Under such circumstances, it would be harder for an information strategy to be optimized.

The possibility that traditional political, economic, and military means may actually vitiate information strategies suggests the need to think through the problems in question prior to selecting which tools of statecraft to employ. If the situation seems to call intuitively for military involvement, or economic suasion, the tendency to seek out counterintuitive solutions (i.e., the use of information as an alternative to the use of force) will be diminished. This is related to the

---

[1]For elaboration of what we mean by an RDA, see Arquilla and Ronfeldt (1997, Ch. 19, and 1998b).

phenomenon that Herbert Simon (1982) called "satisficing"—searching out alternatives for a limited time, then settling on the first acceptable option. Unless decisionmakers habituate themselves to thinking about the possibility of using information first, in lieu of sanctions or military action, it will be all too easy to "satisfice" by settling on old, familiar policy options.

We are not arguing that political, economic, and military power are passé. Rather, we are suggesting that decisionmakers be encouraged to develop a new turn of mind—one more open to thinking about information strategy earlier, and more often. Otherwise, the older tools of statecraft may be unduly relied upon, and possibly employed inappropriately or ineffectively. The added benefit of first employing information strategy is that it will rarely impede later use of other political, economic, or military measures. But first using armies or economic sanctions may make it impossible to use information strategy later to reach either the leaders or mass publics of the other party in some international negotiation or dispute.

Ultimately, information strategy will become an attractive choice for the decisionmaker only after it has been cultivated and developed sufficiently. The challenge is to begin flexing this new, sensory musculature of statecraft that holds so much promise. In this regard, we have mentioned that there are two fundamental approaches to information strategy. The first recognizes the continuing importance of the traditional political, economic, and military dimensions of grand strategy, and seeks to employ information in complementary ways, as an adjunct of each of the traditional dimensions—as in the case of using advanced information technologies and network-centric organizational designs to enhance military effectiveness. The second approach proposes that information is itself in the process of becoming its own distinct dimension of grand strategy—e.g., it is capable of being employed *in lieu of* field armies or economic sanctions. Getting both approaches right in their own times—and making an effective transition from the first to the second over time—are major challenges that lie ahead.

U.S. HEGEMONY REQUIRED TO CONSOLIDATE THE NOOSPHERE?

The information revolution is full of paradoxes and ambivalencies for the United States. It enhances our country's capabilities to deal with others, but it also amplifies our vulnerabilities—the American infosphere presents the richest target set of all. It benefits our worldwide technological edge and ideational appeal and thus makes others look to the United States for leadership—but the prospect of U.S. hegemony and "information imperialism" may also arouse fear and concern. When conflict occurs, it makes us better able to organize and manage security coalitions in which we can share sensitive information for common security—but this also raises the risks of misuse and misconduct by semi-trusted friends or allies. How are Americans to work their way through these paradoxes and ambivalencies?

Where balance-of-power dynamics persist and prevail, so will realpolitik—and neither a global noosphere nor noopolitik will spread sufficiently to guide the course of world politics. Americans thus face a choice: whether to persist in the exercise of classic power politics, as leading powers normally do, or to embrace and hasten the rise of a new paradigm. Noopolitik will not be readily adopted among states if the United States, as the world's leading power, stresses power balancing games above all else (or if it tries to withdraw from these games entirely). To the contrary, heavy, though in some respects redirected, U.S. engagement, may be essential for noopolitik to spread. In our view, America stands to benefit from the rise of the noosphere and noopolitik—and should begin to work to shape it.

It may take some exercise of hegemonic power to foster the development of a global noosphere. Much as classic theories of trade openness depend on a benign hegemon to keep markets open and provide "public goods" (like freedom of the seas), so, too, noopolitik may need a "hegemonic stability theory" of its own—especially if the rise of noopolitik necessitates a permanent disturbance of the balance of power that proponents of realpolitiks so closely guard and relish.[2] In particular, a benevolent hegemon may be needed so that

---

[2]It should be noted that a body of thought holds that efforts to achieve hegemony cause their own cycles of conflict and destruction (Gilpin, 1981; Goldstein, 1988; and

NGOs, individual activists, and others, have the space to build the networked fabric of a global civil society—and a noosphere.

But is there not ultimately some contradiction between the consolidation of a global noosphere and the persistence of the hegemon who works to implant it? Once its catalytic/midwife roles have been completed, does the hegemon just "wither away"? Shouldn't it? Or is continued hegemony needed to sustain and safeguard the noosphere? Just how robust will a noosphere be on its own? And if it is but an artifact of some kind of hegemony, does this mean that noopolitik depends on a continuance of realpolitik at its base? Because, after all, the hegemon, by definition, is the most overarchingly powerful state. These questions and issues bear future inquiry.

Could the United States serve in this hegemonic capacity to good effect? If so, we should cease letting the threat of a "digital Pearl Harbor" be a main metaphor for our strategic thinking and shift to an equally classic, but positive, metaphor along the lines of a "Manifest Destiny" for the information age.

Modelski, 1987). All offer critiques of any form of hegemony, although Modelski considers that hegemony might be a good thing.

BIBLIOGRAPHY

Anderson, Benedict, *Imagined Communities: Reflections on the Origin and Spread of Nationalism*, Revised Edition, New York: Verso, 1991.

Anderson, Robert, and Norman Shapiro, "Deployable Local Networks to Reduce Conflict," in Steve Bankes, Carl Builder, et al., "Seizing the Moment: Harnessing the Information Technologies," *The Information Society*, Vol. 8, No. 3, July–September 1992, pp. 26–30. (Also available as RAND N-3336-RC, 1992.)

Anderson, Robert H., Phillip M. Feldman, Scott Gerwehr, Brian Houghton, Richard Mesic, John D. Pinder, Jeff Rothenberg, and James Chiesa, *Establishing Minimum Essential Information Infrastructure for U.S. Defense Systems*, Santa Monica, Calif.: RAND, forthcoming.

Angell, Norman, *The Great Illusion*, New York: G. P. Putnam, 1913.

Arquilla, John, "Between a Rock and a Hard-Drive: Export Controls on Supercomputers," *The Nonproliferation Review*, Vol. 3, No. 2, Winter 1996, pp. 55–61.

Arquilla, John, "Ethics and Information Warfare," in Zalmay Khalilzad and John White, eds., *Strategic Appraisal: The Changing Role of Information in Warfare*, Santa Monica, Calif.: RAND, forthcoming.

Arquilla, John, and Solomon M. Karmel, "Welcome to the Revolution . . . in Chinese Military Affairs," *Defense Analysis*, Vol. 13, No. 3, Autumn 1997, pp. 255–270.

Arquilla, John, and David Ronfeldt, *The Advent of Netwar*, Santa Monica, Calif.: RAND, MR-789-OSD, 1996a.

Arquilla, John, and David Ronfeldt, "Information, Power, and Grand Strategy: In Athena's Camp," in Stuart J. D. Schwartzstein, ed., *The Information Revolution and National Security: Dimensions and Directions*, Washington, D.C.: Center for International and Strategic Studies, 1996b, pp. 132–180.

Arquilla, John, and David Ronfeldt, "Preparing for Information-Age Conflict, Part I: Conceptual and Organizational Dimensions," *Information, Communication, and Society*, Vol. 1, No. 1, Spring 1998a, pp. 1–22.

Arquilla, John, and David Ronfeldt, "Preparing for Information-Age Conflict, Part II: Doctrinal and Strategic Dimensions," *Information, Communication, and Society*, Vol. 1, No. 2, Summer 1998b, pp. 121–143.

Arquilla, John, and David Ronfeldt, eds., *In Athena's Camp: Preparing for Conflict in the Information Age*, Santa Monica, Calif.: RAND, MR-880-OSD/RC, 1997.

Bankes, Steve, Carl Builder, et al., "Seizing the Moment: Harnessing the Information Technologies," *The Information Society*, Vol. 8, No. 3, July–September 1992, pp. 1–51. (Also available as RAND N-3336-RC, 1992.)

Bateson, Gregory, *Steps to An Ecology of Mind*, New York: Ballantine, 1972.

Bell, Daniel, "Teletext and Technology: New Networks of Knowledge and Information in Post-Industrial Society," *Encounter,* April 1977, pp. 9–29.

Bellah, Robert N., Richard Madsen, William M. Sullivan, Ann Swindler, and Steven M. Tipton, *Habits of the Heart: Individualism and Commitment in American Life*, updated edition, Berkeley, Calif.: University of California Press, 1996.

Beniger, James R., *The Control Revolution: Technological and Economic Origins of the Information Society*, Cambridge, Mass.: Harvard University Press, 1986.

Boulding, Elise, *Building a Global Civic Culture: Education for an Interdependent World*, New York: Teachers College Press, Teachers College, Columbia University, 1988.

Boulding, Elise, "Ethnicity and New Constitutive Orders," in Jeremy Brecher, John Brown Childs, and Jill Cutler, eds., *Global Visions: Beyond the New World Order*, Boston, Mass.: South End Press, 1993, pp. 213–231.

Brand, Stewart, *The Media Lab: Inventing the Future at MIT*, New York: Penguin Books, 1989.

Brin, David, *The Transparent Society: Will Technology Force Us to Choose Between Privacy and Freedom?* Reading, Mass.: Addison-Wesley, 1998.

Brzezinski, Zbigniew, *The Grand Chessboard: American Primacy and Its Geostrategic Imperatives*, New York: Basic Books, 1997.

Burt, Richard, Olin Robison, and Barry Fulton, *Reinventing Diplomacy in the Information Age: A Report of the CSIS Advisory Panel on Diplomacy in the Information Age*, Washington, D.C.: Center for Strategic and International Studies, 1998.

Cambone, Stephen A., *Kodak Moments, Inescapable Momentum, and the World Wide Web: Has the Infocomm Revolution Transformed Diplomacy?* McLean, Va.: The Center for Information Strategy and Policy, Science Applications International Corporation, 1996.

Campen, Alan, Douglas Dearth, and R. T. Goodden, eds., *Cyberwar: Security, Strategy and Conflict in the Information Age*, Fairfax, Va.: AFCEA International Press, 1996.

Capra, Fritjof, *The Web of Life: A New Scientific Understanding of Living Systems*, New York: Anchor Books, 1996.

Castells, Manuel, *The Rise of the Network Society (The Information Age: Economy, Society and Culture, Volume I)*, Malden, Mass.: Blackwell Publishers, 1996.

Castells, Manuel, *The Power of Identity (The Information Age: Economy, Society and Culture, Volume II)*, Malden, Mass.: Blackwell Publishers, 1997.

Cebrowski, Arthur K., and John J. Garstka, "Network-Centric Warfare: Its Origins and Future," *United States Naval Institute Proceedings*, January 1998, pp. 28–35.

Clark, Ann Marie, Elisabeth J. Friedman, and Kathryn Hochstetler, "The Sovereign Limits of Global Civil Society: A Comparison of NGO Participation in UN World Conferences on the Environment, Human Rights, and Women," *World Politics*, Vol. 51, No. 1, October 1998, pp. 1–35.

Cleaver, Harry, "The Zapatista Effect: The Internet and the Rise of an Alternative Political Fabric," *Journal of International Affairs*, Vol. 51, No. 2, Spring 1998, pp. 621–640.

Cobb, Jennifer, "A Globe, Clothing Itself with a Brain," *Wired*, 3.06, June 1995, pp. 108–113.

Cobb, Jennifer, *Cybergrace: The Search for God in the Digital World*, New York: Crown Publishers, 1998.

Cooper, Jeffrey R., *The Emerging Infosphere: Some Thoughts on Implications of the "Information Revolution,"* McLean, Va.: Center for Information Strategy and Policy, Science Applications International Corporation, 1997.

Danitz, Tiffany, and Warren P. Strobel, *Networking Dissent: Burmese Cyberactivists Promote Nonviolent Struggle Using the Internet*, forthcoming.

Dawkins, Richard, *The Selfish Gene*, New York: Oxford University Press, 1989.

De Caro, Charles, "Softwar," in Alan Campen, Douglas Dearth, and R. T. Goodden, eds., *Cyberwar: Security, Strategy and Conflict in the Information Age*, Fairfax, Va.: AFCEA International Press, 1996, pp. 203–218.

De Seversky, Alexander, *Victory Through Air Power*, New York: Simon and Schuster, 1942.

Defense Science Board, *Report of the Defense Science Board Task Force on Information Warfare—Defense*, Washington, D.C.: Office of the Under Secretary of Defense for Acquisition and Technology, November 1977.

Dehio, Ludwig, *The Precarious Balance,* New York: Alfred A. Knopf, 1961.

Der Derian, James, "Speed Pollution," *Wired,* Vol. 4, No. 5, May 1996, p. 121.

Dertouzos, Michael, *What Will Be: How the New World of Information Will Change Our Lives,* San Francisco: HarperCollins, 1997.

Douhet, Giulio, *The Command of the Air,* translated by Dino Ferrari, New York: Coward-McCann, 1942.

Dyson, Esther, *Release 2.0: A Design for Living in the Digital Age,* New York: Broadway Books, 1997.

Frederick, Howard, "Computer Networks and the Emergence of Global Civil Society," in Linda M. Harasim, ed., *Global Networks: Computers and International Communication,* Cambridge, Mass.: The MIT Press, 1993a, pp. 283–295.

Frederick, Howard, *Global Communication and International Relations,* Belmont, Calif.: Wadsworth Publishing Co., 1993b.

Gibson, William, *Neuromancer,* New York: Ace Books, 1984.

Gilpin, Robert, *War & Change in World Politics,* Cambridge, Mass.: Cambridge University Press, 1981.

Golden, James R., "Economics and National Strategy: Convergence, Global Networks, and Cooperative Competition," *The Washington Quarterly,* Vol. 16, No. 3, Summer 1993, pp. 91–113.

Goldstein, Joshua, *Long Cycles: Prosperity and War in the Modern Age,* New Haven: Yale University Press, 1988.

Gompert, David, *Right Makes Might: Freedom and Power in the Information Age,* McNair Paper 59, Washington, D.C.: NDU Press, May 1998.

Goodman, Seymour, Peter Wolcott, and Grey Burkhart, *Building on Basics: An Examination of High-Performance Computing Export*

Control Policy in the 1990s, Stanford: Center for International Security and Arms Control, 1995.

Harasim, Linda M., ed., *Global Networks: Computers and International Communication,* Cambridge, Mass.: The MIT Press, 1993.

Hopf, Ted, "The Promise of Constructivism in International Relations Theory," *International Security,* Vol. 23, No. 1, Summer 1998, pp. 171–200.

Hundley, Richard O., and Robert H. Anderson, *Security in Cyberspace: An Emerging Challenge for Society,* Santa Monica, Calif.: RAND, P-7893, 1994.

Huntington, Samuel P., "America's Changing Strategic Interests," *Survival,* January/February 1991.

Huntington, Samuel P., *The Clash of Civilizations and the Remaking of World Order,* New York: Simon and Schuster, 1996.

Ikenberry, G. John, "New Grand Strategy Uses Lofty and Material Desires," *The Los Angeles Times,* July 12, 1998, Sunday Opinion Section, pp. M1, M6.

Jervis, Robert, *System Effects: Complexity in Political and Social Life,* Princeton, N.J.: Princeton University Press, 1997.

Joffe, Joseph, "How America Does It," *Foreign Affairs,* Vol. 76, No. 5, September/October 1997, pp. 13–27.

Kedzie, Christopher R., *Communication and Democracy: Coincident Revolutions and the Emergent Dictator's Dilemma,* Santa Monica, Calif.: RAND, RGSD-127, 1997.

Kelly, Kevin, *Out of Control: The Rise of Neo-Biological Civilization,* New York: Addison-Wesley Publishing Company, 1994.

Kennedy, Paul, *The Rise and Fall of the Great Powers,* New York: Random House, 1987.

Keohane, Robert, *After Hegemony,* Princeton: Princeton University Press, 1984.

Keohane, Robert O., and Joseph S. Nye, *Power and Interdependence: World Politics in Transition,* Little, Brown and Company, Boston, 1977.

Keohane, Robert O., and Joseph S. Nye, Jr., "Power and Interdependence in the Information Age," *Foreign Affairs,* Vol. 77, No. 5, September/October 1998, pp. 81–94.

Keohane, Robert O., and Joseph S. Nye, Jr., eds., *Transnational Relations and World Politics,* Cambridge, Mass.: Harvard University Press, 1972.

Kissinger, Henry, *Diplomacy,* New York: Simon & Schuster, 1994.

Kobrin, Stephen J., "The MAI and the Clash of Globalizations," *Foreign Policy,* No. 112, Fall 1998, pp. 97–109.

Kotkin, Joel, *Tribes: How Race, Religion and Identity Determine Success in the New Global Economy,* New York: Random House, 1993.

Kumon, Shumpei, and Izumi Aizu, "Co-Emulation: The Case for a Global Hypernetwork Society, in Linda M. Harasim, ed., *Global Networks: Computers and International Communication,* Cambridge, Mass.: The MIT Press, 1993, pp. 311–326.

Lakoff, George, and Mark Johnson, *Metaphors We Live By,* Chicago: The University of Chicago Press, 1980.

Larson, Eric V., *Casualties and Consensus: The Historical Role of Casualties in Domestic Support for U.S. Military Operations,* Santa Monica, Calif.: RAND, MR-726-RC, 1996.

Libicki, Martin, "Information Warfare: A Brief Guide to Defense Preparedness," *Physics Today,* September 1997, pp. 40–45.

Libicki, Martin C., "Information War, Information Peace," *Journal of International Affairs,* Vol. 51, No. 2, Spring 1998, pp. 411–428.

Libicki, Martin C., *Illuminating Tomorrow's War,* Washington, D.C.: NDU Press, forthcoming.

Lipset, Seymour Martin, *Political Man,* New York: Doubleday, 1960.

Lynch, Aaron, *Thought Contagion: How Belief Spreads Through Society*, New York: Basic Books, 1996.

Manheim, Jarol, *Strategic Public Diplomacy and American Foreign Policy: The Evolution of Influence*, New York: Oxford University Press, 1994.

Mathews, Jessica, "Power Shift," *Foreign Affairs*, Vol. 76, No. 1, January/February 1997, pp. 50–66.

Maynes, Charles William, "'Principled' Hegemony," *World Policy Journal*, Vol. XIV, No. 3, Fall 1997, pp. 31–36.

McLuhan, Marshall, Quentin Fiore, and Jerome Agel, *The Medium Is the Massage: An Inventory of Effects*, New York: Random House, 1967.

Mearsheimer, John, "The False Promise of International Institutions," *International Security*, Vol. 19, No. 3, Winter 1994–1995, pp. 5–49.

Metzl, Jamie, "Information Intervention," *Foreign Affairs*, Vol. 76, No. 6, November/December 1997, pp. 15–20.

Modelski, George, *Long Cycles in World Politics*, Seattle: University of Washington Press, 1987.

Molander, Roger C., Andrew S. Riddile, and Peter A. Wilson, *Strategic Information Warfare: A New Face of War*, Santa Monica, Calif.: RAND, MR-661-OSD, 1996.

Morgenthau, Hans, *Politics Among Nations*, New York: Alfred A. Knopf, 1948.

North, Douglass, *Structure and Change in Economic History*, New York: Norton, 1981.

Nye, Joseph S., "Independence and Interdependence," *Foreign Policy*, No. 22, Spring 1976, pp. 130–161.

Nye, Joseph S., *Bound to Lead: The Changing Nature of American Power*, New York: Basic Books, 1990.

Nye, Joseph S., and William A. Owens, "America's Information Edge," *Foreign Affairs*, Vol. 75, No. 2, March/April 1996, pp. 20–36.

Ohmae, Kenichi, *The Borderless World: Power and Strategy in the Interlinked Economy*, New York: HarperBusiness, 1990.

Ohmae, Kenichi, *The End of the Nation-State: The Rise of Regional Economies*, New York: The Free Press, 1995.

Pennington, Nancy, and Reid Hastie, "Evidence Evaluation in Complex Decision Making," *Journal of Personality and Social Psychology*, Vol. 51, No. 2, 1986, pp. 242–258.

Perrow, Charles, *Normal Accidents: Living with High-Risk Technologies*, New York: Basic Books, 1984.

Pfaltzgraff, Robert, and Richard Shultz, *War in the Information Age*, London: Brassey's, 1997.

Price, Richard, "Reversing the Gun Sights: Transnational Civil Society Targets Land Mines," *International Organization*, Vol. 52, No. 3, Summer 1998, pp. 613–644.

The Project on the Advocacy of U.S. Interests Abroad, *Equipped for the Future: Managing U.S. Foreign Affairs in the 21st Century*, Washington, D.C.: The Henry L. Stimson Center, October 1998.

Quarterman, John S., *The Matrix: Computer Networks and Conferencing Systems Worldwide*, Bedford, Mass.: Digital Press, Digital Equipment Corporation, 1990.

Quarterman, John S., "The Global Matrix of Minds," in Linda M. Harasim, ed., *Global Networks: Computers and International Communication*, Cambridge, Mass.: The MIT Press, 1993, pp. 35–56.

Radvanyi, Janos, *Psychological Operations and Political Warfare*, New York: Praeger, 1990.

Report of the President's Commission on Critical Infrastructure Protection, Washington, D.C.: U.S. Government Printing Office, 1997. Available online at http://www.pccip.gov/.

Rheingold, Howard, *The Virtual Community: Homesteading on the Electronic Frontier*, Reading, Mass.: Addison-Wesley, 1993.

Ronfeldt, David, "Cyberocracy Is Coming," *The Information Society*, Vol. 8, No. 4, 1992, pp. 243–296. (Available as RAND RP-222.)

Ronfeldt, David, *Tribes, Institutions, Markets, Networks: A Framework About Societal Evolution*, Santa Monica, Calif.: RAND, P-7967, 1996.

Ronfeldt, David, John Arquilla, Graham Fuller, and Melissa Fuller, *The Zapatista "Social Netwar" in Mexico*, Santa Monica, Calif.: RAND, MR-994-A, 1998.

Ronfeldt, David, and Monica Ortíz de Oppermann, *Mexican Immigration, U.S. Investment, and U.S.-Mexican Relations*, Santa Monica, Calif.: RAND, JRI-08, 1990.

Rosecrance, Richard, *Rise of the Trading State*, New York: Basic Books, 1984.

Rosenau, James N., "Patterned Chaos in Global Life: Structure and Process in the Two Worlds of Global Politics," *International Political Science Review*, Vol. 9, No. 4, 1988, pp. 327–364.

Rosenau, James N., *Turbulence in World Politics: A Theory of Change and Continuity*, Princeton: Princeton University Press, 1990.

Rosenau, James N., "The Relocation of Authority in a Shrinking World," *Comparative Politics*, April 1992, pp. 253–272.

Rothkopf, David J., "Cyberpolitik: The Changing Nature of Power in the Information Age," *Journal of International Affairs*, Vol. 51, No. 2, Spring 1998, pp. 325–359.

Ruggie, John Gerard, "What Makes the World Hang Together? Neo-Utilitarianism and the Social Constructivist Challenge," *International Organization*, Vol. 52, No. 4, Autumn 1998, pp. 855–885.

Sanderson, Stephen K., *Social Transformations: A General Theory of Historical Development*, Cambridge, Mass.: Blackwell, 1995.

Sassen, Saskia, *The Global City: New York, London, Tokyo*, Princeton: Princeton University Press, 1991.

Sassen, Saskia, *Globalization and Its Discontents*, New York: The New Press, 1998.

Schudson, Michael, *The Good Citizen: A History of American Civic Life*, New York: The Free Press, 1998.

Schumpeter, Joseph, *A History of Economic Analysis*, New York: Oxford University Press, 1954.

Scott, James C., *Seeing Like a State: How Certain Schemes to Improve the Human Condition Have Failed*, New Haven: Yale University Press, 1998.

Shultz, George, "New Realities and New Ways of Thinking," *Foreign Affairs*, Spring 1985, pp. 705–721.

Shultz, George, "Diplomacy in the Information Age," in United States Institute for Peace, *Keynote Addresses from the Virtual Diplomacy Conference*, Peaceworks No. 18, Washington, D.C.: United States Institute for Peace, 1997, pp. 12–16.

Simmons, P. J., "Learning to Live with NGOs," *Foreign Policy*, No. 112, Fall 1998, pp. 82–96.

Simon, Herbert, *Models of Bounded Rationality*, Cambridge, Mass.: MIT Press, 1982.

Skolnikoff, Eugene B., *The Elusive Transformation: Science, Technology, and the Evolution of International Politics*, Princeton: Princeton University Press, 1993.

Slaughter, Anne-Marie, "The New World Order," *Foreign Affairs*, Vol. 76, No. 5, September/October 1997, pp. 183–197.

Smith, George, "An Electronic Pearl Harbor? Not Likely," *Issues in Science and Technology*, Vol. 15, No. 1, Fall 1998, pp. 68–73.

Solomon, Richard H., "The Information Revolution and International Conflict Management," in United States Institute for Peace, *Keynote Addresses from the Virtual Diplomacy Conference*, Peaceworks No. 18, Washington, D.C.: United States Institute for Peace, 1997, pp. 1–5.

Stein, George, "Information Warfare," *Airpower Journal*, Spring 1995, pp. 30–39.

Strange, Susan, *States and Markets*, London: Pinter Publishers Limited, 1988.

Szafranski, Richard, "Neo-Cortical Warfare? The Acme of Skill," *Military Review*, November 1994, pp. 41–55.

Szafranski, Richard, "A Theory of Information Warfare: Preparing for 2020," *Airpower Journal*, Spring 1995, pp. 56–65.

Teilhard de Chardin, Pierre, *The Making of a Mind: Letters of a Soldier-Priest, 1914–1919*, New York: Harper and Row, 1961.

Teilhard de Chardin, Pierre, *The Future of Man*, Translated from the French [1959] by Norman Denny, New York: Harper & Row, 1964.

Teilhard de Chardin, Pierre, *The Phenomenon of Man*, With an Introduction by Julian Huxley, Translated from the French [1955] by Bernard Wall, New York: Harper & Row, 1965.

Tenner, Edward, *Why Things Bite Back: Technology and the Revenge of Unintended Consequences*, New York: Knopf, 1996.

Thomas, Timothy, "The Threat of Information Warfare: Russian Perspectives," in Robert Pfaltzgraff and Richard Shultz, eds., *War in the Information Age*, London: Brassey's, 1997.

Toffler, Alvin, and Heidi Toffler, *War and Anti-War: Survival at the Dawn of the Twenty-first Century*, Boston: Little, Brown and Company, 1993.

Toffler, Alvin, and Heidi Toffler, "The New Intangibles," in John Arquilla and David Ronfeldt, eds., *In Athena's Camp: Preparing for Conflict in the Information Age*, Santa Monica, Calif.: RAND, MR-880-OSD/RC, 1997, pp. viii–xxiv.

Vlahos, Michael, "Entering the Infosphere," *Journal of International Affairs*, Vol. 51, No. 2, Spring 1998, pp. 497–525.

von Mises, Ludwig, *Theory and History: An Interpretation of Social and Economic Revolution*, New Haven: Yale University Press, 1957.

Waltz, Kenneth, *Theory of International Politics*, Reading, Mass.: Addison-Wesley, 1979.

Ware, Willis H., *The Cyber-Posture of the National Information Infrastructure*, Santa Monica, Calif.: RAND, MR-976-OSTP, 1998.

Weigley, Russell, *The American Way of War*, New York: Macmillan, 1973.

Wilson, Edward O., *Consilience: The Unity of Knowledge*, New York: Alfred A. Knopf, 1998.

Worsley, Peter, *Knowledges: Culture, Counterculture, Subculture*, New York: The New Press, 1997.

Wright, Robert, *Three Scientists and Their Gods: Looking for Meaning in an Age of Information*, New York: Harper & Row, 1989.

Wriston, Walter, "Bits, Bytes, and Diplomacy," *Foreign Affairs*, Vol. 76, No. 5, September/October 1997, pp. 172–182.

Zakaria, Fareed, "The Rise of Illiberal Democracy," *Foreign Affairs*, Vol. 76, No. 6, November/December 1997, pp. 22–43.